BEING THE
Church
in a Post-Pandemic World

Game Changers for the Post-Pandemic Church

Kay Kotan

Foreword by Rodney Thomas Smothers

Market
Square
BOOKS

Being The Church
in a Post-Pandemic World

books@marketsquarebooks.com
P.O. Box 23664 Knoxville, Tennessee 37933
ISBN: 978-1-950899-22-7
Library of Congress Control Number: 2021936110

Printed and Bound in the United States of America
Cover Illustration & Book Design ©2021 Market Square Publishing, LLC
Publisher: Kevin Slimp
Editor: Kristin Lighter
Post-Process Editor: Ken Rochelle

Scripture quotations used with permission from:

"We're not going back to normal."[*]

Gideon Lichfield

* Gideon Lichfield, *MIT Technology Review,* March 2020.

Table of Contents

Foreword

Rev. Dr. Rodney Thomas Smothers

Kay writes with a voice of a prophet, and she is a witness and warrior. Her perceptions and predictions make this resource both a tool and a tactical manual. When she writes, she is correct; "Most of us could have never imagined the life we encountered in 2020." Kay's pronouncement that life will never be the same – our new reality is yet to be determined – is a realistic assessment of how we need to prepare as leaders. One thing is certain as Kay writes, "We must show up in different and new ways."

The Eight Game Changers we must embrace to thrive are skillfully laid out in this resource as we are invited to adapt to emerging challenges, innovate and live into adaptive change. Kay shows us the way by helping us navigate disruptions as opportunities to be awakened to a need for change at every level of our future attempts to engage unfamiliar seasons of ministry that awaits us. She leads us into new insights regarding how the present disruptions are opportunities to adjust our metrics from attendance to engagement, where discipleship, service, worship and evangelism become re-envisioned.

In this resource, Kay assists us to recover the importance of becoming a healthy, vital, culturally relevant church.

1

She teaches us how to embrace being visionary, spiritually grounded, highly committed, innovative, resilient and courageous. At the end of each chapter, reflection questions make this resource valuable for both individual and team resourcing. Kay then takes us on a fresh and insightful discussion about flexibility and adaptability as we seek a pathway to the future. This new pathway realigns purpose, people and processes around flexibility and shared risk.

The heart of this resource is found in what Kay defines as the fifteen shifts that lead us to become highly relational churches that reach new people in the post-pandemic world. As if that is not enough, her chapter on Vision, teaches vision as a transformation bridge that charts a course of a vision-inspired and vision-lead process that not only challenges our past assumptions, but gives us the tools to abide in new spaces that are vision-driven on purpose.

Kay gives us a rich perspective on "the why," then teaches us "the how," like a Master Guide inspires her students to take things to the next level. Commitment, innovation, resilience and courage frame the Call To Action that she skillfully gives us as a GPS for our present location and our future destinations. This resource will be used in classrooms, conference rooms, congregational development seminars and as a personal guidebook for equipping Post-pandemic Strategies for many years to come.

Rev. Dr. Rodney Thomas Smothers
Lead Pastor, Grace United Methodist Church and
Director of Leadership and Congregational Development
The Baltimore – Washington Conference of The United Methodist Church

CHAPTER ONE

The Pandemic's Arrival

*"To be hopeful means to be uncertain about the future,
to be tender toward possibilities, to be dedicated to change
all the way down to the bottom of your heart."*

Rebecca Solnit
Writer & Historian

Most of us could never have imagined the life we encountered beginning in March 2020. Our world essentially shut down for a time. Only essential workers were providing for those of us in lock-down. People were hunkered down in their homes, spending more time with family and roommates than ever before. Students transitioned to virtual learning. Seemingly overnight, employees shifted from fighting the rush hour traffic commute to working from home.

Many of us began spending hours a day on digital platforms, conducting business that was once conducted in person. Families began cooking at home. Kitchen tables became multi-functional spaces for eating, virtual school, and digital boardrooms. Amazon was flooded with online orders. Curbside pickup for groceries and restaurants surged. There were shortages of everyday products, such as disinfectant wipes and sprays, paper towels, and toilet paper. We were unable to gather with loved ones. Airlines and cruise ships came to a screeching halt. Events were canceled. Special occasions such as graduations, weddings, family reunions, long-awaited vacations were postponed or canceled. Churches closed their facilities. Funerals were foregone or postponed indefinitely.

A major and sudden global stock market crash began on February 20, 2020, thankfully ended (for the most part) on April 7, 2020. The crash was the fastest fall in global stock markets in financial history, and the most devastating crash since the Wall Street Crash of 1929. Covid-19 (aka Coronavirus) struck the world with vengeance. Who could have ever imagined that in a matter of days our world would be turned upside down?

Since March 2020, when our lives were turned inside out, many have craved returning to the ways things once were. We continually heard comments like, "I can't wait to get back to normal!" People longed for the life pre-Covid. They hungered for their old routine. While the mundane day-to-day life may not have been perfect, at least people knew what to expect. There was comfort in the routine and the known. And they just wanted to go back NOW.

Life during Covid was uncertain. There were too many questions left unanswered. Conflicting news left people wondering what the truth really was.

- How bad is it really? How long will this last?
- How many will be infected?

- How many will lose their lives?
- Is this cough Covid?
- Will my loved ones remain healthy?
- When will a vaccine become available for all?
- Will the vaccine be safe to take?
- What long-term effects will this have on my health, my job, my family, my children's education and the economy?
- When will I be able to see my loved ones in long-term care facilities?

As the quarantine and stay-at-home orders lingered, the population grew even more isolated. Loneliness, anxiety, abuse, addiction, and more were on the rise. "When will it end? When will my life as I once knew it return?"

> Reality check: Life will never be the same. The world, and therefore our lives, have changed forever. There is no going back. Our new reality is yet to be determined. The effects will take some time to settle in. Adjustments will continue to have a ripple effect for years to come.

The time between one season ending (pre-Covid) and a new season beginning (post-Covid) is referred to as a *liminal time*. In Susan Beaumont's book, *How to Lead When You Don't Know Where You're Going,*[1] he writes:

---

[1] Susan Beaumont, *How to Lead When You Don't Know Where You're Going: Leading in a Liminal Season,* Rowman & Littlefield Publishers, Inc., 2019.

Liminality refers to a quality of ambiguity or disorientation that occurs during transition. It is described as a time when a person or group of people is in between something that has ended and something else that is not yet ready to begin. Transition experiences follow a predictable pattern that involves separation, liminality, and reorientation.

We know the church as we knew it before the pandemic no longer exists. Yet, we do not know what the church of the future will be. One thing we know for sure is that it will be different.

It needs to be different. In fact, it has to be different! If we are to be the church to reach new people, we must show up in different and new ways. We must shed the methods that no longer serve the church and be open to being the church in new (and yet to be determined) ways. After we exit the stage of liminality, we will begin the time of reorientation.

We would all like to know where we are headed, what the future will look like, how it will be different, and what we will be doing. Unfortunately, that's just not possible. If we can keep from going back to the way things were, we will want to reorient as soon as possible. We want to race to reorientation when the time is not yet ready. As much as we want to sprint towards reorientation, we must also acknowledge that even this will be another difficult phase of adjusting, re-learning, and adapting. Still another season of being uncomfortable.

We are in divergent times. Things are developing differently, or perhaps in different directions. While we would all love the perceived certainty we had in January 2020, we must face the reality of where our feet are planted, acknowledging we will need to move in unknown directions in the moments, days, and years to come.

In thinking about these divergent or liminal times, there is another reality to consider. The pre-pandemic church might have been comfortable, but as a whole it was certainly not entirely fruitful. I could share heartbreaking stories of working with churches and holding the mirror up to the leadership who were absolutely shocked with what they saw. They knew there were fewer people, but never realized the totality of decline because of its slow trickle. It seems like almost no one had paid much attention to long-term trends. Mostly, church leaders were trying to pay the bills and keep the existing flock happy. Too frequently, we were not paying attention to the bigger picture: the missional effectiveness of the church. The pandemic certainly didn't cause the decline of the church, but it made the decline more obvious and accelerated the decline for those that were already struggling. Therefore, the pandemic has created a sense of urgency for some churches to address their missional ineffectiveness. Mind you, these churches would not frame their concern as missional ineffectiveness, it would likely be cited as the inability to pay the bills.

The Initial Rally Cry

As church leaders, this pandemic has resulted in both challenges and opportunities. Leaders' initial responses were a true rally cry to meet the emerging and sometimes present needs. Many churches pivoted to online worship for the first time out of necessity. One Sunday they were worshiping in-person. The next week, they were suddenly online. Care teams of both clergy and laity were assembled to make weekly phone calls to check in on members. Resources for children and youth ministries were created and distributed electronically or delivered to doorsteps. Church food pantries ramped up to meet the growing needs of families who suddenly found themselves without paychecks. Church parking lots were turned into Covid testing sites.

Indeed, the church rose to the occasion. The church adapted. As a result, most church members felt well cared for. Those who had once been resistant to technology (and specifically online worship) were now watching online worship via cell phones, laptops, tablets, or dialing in to listen and participate. Individuals, businesses, and organizations were all catapulted technologically into the future like no other time in ministry, almost overnight. Church staff and ministry leaders learned new skills and expanded – or even completely changed – their job descriptions to meet the new demands of virtual ministry. Music was prerecorded. Vocalists recorded their individual voice, which was then mixed with other voices via the magic of technology so the congregation could still enjoy a choir anthem or quartet. Individuals recorded liturgy, prayers, children's moments, announcements, and sermons on their phones and tablets. Then, almost magically,through the power of technology, one seamless worship experience was produced. About a third of churches initially reported online view counts that surpassed the on-site worship attendance pre-Covid. Clergy and laity alike stepped up in profound ways to be the church in this time of Covid.

The Onset of Weariness

After Easter and Mother's Day, "it" began. Online views and attendance began to slip. Many churches suddenly found themselves in a worship rut ... in a routine that resulted in limited appeal. The novelty and newness of online ministry had worn off. While some were attending multiple services at different churches, a growing number stopped tuning in at all. Many believed the season of Covid might last several weeks or a few months, but surely this would not be a long-term situation. As the weeks grew into months and the number of infected and deaths rose, reality began to sink in – This would be a much longer season than expected. Some began to understand there was no going back. We were struggling with what it meant to step forward, let alone leap forward.

After the initial surge of energy and adaptations faded and the attendance began slipping, weariness began to set in. One can't sustain the ongoing pressures of working outside the comfort zone, home and work routines turned upside down, isolation from friends, family, and staff, increased need for congregational care, and the growing feelings of fear and uncertainty. Pastors frequently shared their frustration in having to suddenly become producers of online experiences (and/or video editors) without any training or experience. They missed the energy of preaching to a live group of people and felt uncomfortable preaching to a camera. Church leaders were scrambling to identify, locate, and purchase the appropriate equipment to offer online ministries. Church staff pivots, job description changes, position eliminations, staff expenses versus declining offerings, staff overworked, staff underworked, and supervising staff virtually all added to clergy weariness. At the very time the church needed to be the most creative, adaptive, innovative, and cutting-edge, we found ourselves (clergy and laity alike) instead buried in a state of weariness.

Adapting vs Innovating

As mentioned previously, the church did indeed adapt. Some adapted better than others. Some were more open to adapting than others. Some adapted more deeply than others. Yet, most of us adapted as best we could. While adapting was needed, adapting is a new strategy without a new vision. Furthermore, we adapted, but did we innovate?

Allow me to offer a distinction between adapting and innovating:

- Adapting is taking something you already have, or is already known, and making it suitable for a new use or new conditions.

- Innovation, on the other hand, is introducing brand new methods, ideas or products. Adapting is more of a technical change. Innovation is adaptive change. A technical change is more mono-focused, having an easily determined fix. A technical change is less complex (often a single issue), takes a shorter time, and is easier to identify and enact a solution. An adaptive change is more complex, multi-layered, has longer term effects, has no easy answers, and often calls us to move outside our comfort zone of knowing, doing, and/or being.

Let's tie adapting and technical change together with an example. Moving on-site worship to an online format resulted in offering the worship we already knew and offered it digitally. The delivery method needed to change. We could locate tech experts who could help us figure out how to take what we were already doing (live worship) and adjust it to new conditions (online worship). It was a single issue that needed to be changed, and we knew what we needed to do (or could find an expert to help us) to make the change happen. Mind you, I never said this was easy! Yet, there was a clear path for the needed change. We took what we already knew (sanctuary worship), adjusted it for a new condition (same worship offered online), and found the already available technology to make it happen quickly (often in less than a week).

Now let's tie innovating and adapting change together with an example. Knowing those who would join online rather than on-site tend to engage and experience things differently, we knew the format used for on-site worship needed to change for an online audience. An image of the pulpit taken from the balcony would feel too impersonal and distant. The engagement time online is normally less than the time people were willing to give on-site. The interactive elements on-site had to be transitioned to a meaningful and engaging virtual experience. We dealt with our "normal" elements like meet and greets, the offering, connection cards, congregational singing, and more with new approaches appropriate for a virtual experience that was still highly relational. We needed to explore moving to a place other than the pulpit or chancel area with tighter camera shots.

Perhaps the reach of people engaging in this new worship experience might be different than those we were reaching with an on-site experience, so we needed to consider how this would affect the music offerings, worship format, sermon subject, style, and length, and how to lead worship without on-site audience interaction. Considering the multiple layers makes the issues even more complex. These issues were too much for one person or expert to solve. To innovate and apply adaptive change means looking long term, further down the field.

We took the same presenting issue as the previous example, then applied innovation and adaptive change to it. The issue was identified as being multi-layered. Several aspects needed to be examined and rethought. This approach was beyond taking the known and applying a different method. This approach was starting from scratch and creating a new experience by tackling multiple elements, approaches, and methods. The desired outcome was unknown. Leaders would have to tap into brand new ways of thinking, planning, and offering worship.

Interruption or Disruption

Let's explore another important distinction the pandemic has presented for our consideration. When we look at the pandemic as an interruption, we are seeing it as a delay. It is as though we hit the pause button, and when the world returns to "normal" we will simply hit the play button again.

12

On the contrary "disruption is a major disturbance, something that changes your plans, interrupts some event or process", or "a break in the action – especially an unplanned and confusing one."[2] When the church sees the pandemic as a disruption, the leaders embrace the opportunity of knowing going back is no longer an option. A disruption allows a church the opportunity to be awakened for the need to change at a much deeper level.

> *I know the plans I have for you,' announces the Lord.*
> *'I want you to enjoy success. I do not plan to harm you.*
> *I will give you hope for the years to come.'*
>
> **Jeremiah 29:11 (NIrV)**

While we all mourn the days of the past for what felt normal and comfortable, churches that embrace this as a time of disruption will likely be the most vital churches in the post-pandemic world. God wants the church to be healthy, vital, growing, and fruitful. We must understand that church health and vitality might look very different in the future.

Effective churches will not look at the average worship attendance as the standard barometer for health. Rather, they will be focusing on engagement. How people are engaging in the church through ministries such as discipleship, service, worship, and evangelism will become the new barometer. This single example of changing how

---

2   "Disruption," https://www.vocabulary.com/dictionary/disruption. Accessed January 22, 2021.

might not be the traits and practices the church embraced pre-pandemic. Yet, I believe these are the traits, habits, and practices that will be required if we are to be the church God is calling us to be in the post-pandemic world.

I believe the two most critical and leading key traits for a healthy, vital, and culturally relevant church in the post-pandemic world will be:

- Flexibility
- Highly relational

Additional traits and practices the church and its leaders will need to embrace include:

- Being visionary
- Being spiritually grounded
- Being highly committed
- Being innovative
- Being resilient
- Being courageous

In the next chapters, you will be introduced to each trait and why each is critical if the church and its leaders plan to be healthy and vital in a post-pandemic world. In addition, in each chapter you will find an example of the trait offered, along with an illustration or story.

At the end of each chapter, you will find questions for you to discuss with other church leaders. After the discussion, you and your leadership team will be asked to provide an assessment of your congregation's response to that particular trait.

Compare the numbers each leader selected in the assessments. Discuss the thoughts behind each assessment and the different lenses and perspectives of the various leaders and what you might learn from each assessment score.

After you and other church leaders have explored all nine traits and practices, answered the questions, and completed the assessments, you will have identified your congregation's strengths, discovered gaps that need to be addressed in order to be a vital post-pandemic church.

I am a big fan of being a continuous and life-long learner. I would love to see more churches embrace this trait especially in their lay and clergy leadership. What better way to stay relevant, missionally focused, and on the leading-edge. However, I have discovered that we United Methodists have become avid learners, but not necessarily avid reflectors or implementers. My prayer is that this resource will become a catalyst for conversation, assessment, action-plan creation, and implementation plans to fill the gaps identified. We do not need more knowledge. Rather, we need to be seekers of knowledge and wisdom that causes us to reflect and implement with new insights and understandings. This will result in our growing closer to Christ and to being the church He is calling, needing, and expecting us to be!

Bottom Line

Friends, this is a rally cry! The pre pandemic church no longer exists. The post-pandemic church is forming. Don't allow this new formation to develop by happenstance nor resist the new formation. Instead, form and develop the post-pandemic church with intentional, strategic steps to be more faithful in fulfilling its disciple-making mission. Grab your leadership team and set off to discover what God is calling your church to become and do in this post-pandemic world. Let's get started!

Questions to Ponder

1. How prepared and open is your congregation's leadership as it applies to becoming a post-pandemic church that is vital and fruitful?

2. How ready and willing do you believe the congregation is to become a vital and fruitful church, no matter what changes need to be made for this to become reality?

3. How deep is the sense of urgency for making necessary shifts towards becoming a more effective church in reaching the post-pandemic world?

4. What is your prayer (personally, congregationally, community, and the Kingdom) as you begin your journey into this resource and how God might move as a result?

Current Church Assessment

In considering your current congregation:

How would you rate its current abilities and results in being a vital, effective congregation in this post-pandemic world? Circle the number below that best represents its ability and results.

0=No Ability and/or Results in Being Vital & Effective

10=Excellent Ability and Results in Being Vital & Effective

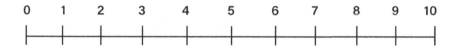

CHAPTER THREE

Flexibility

For last year's words
belong to last year's language.
And next year's words
await another voice.

T.S. Eliot

This quote from T.S. Eliot focuses me on the paradigm shift
that is emerging.

We will not return to normal; we have the opportunity to
listen to the voice of God's Spirit.

Bishop Michael McKee
North Texas Conference UMC

I recently asked a question on my Facebook page that stirred all sorts of interesting and thoughtful comments and interactions. I simply asked,

"What do you believe will be the top three traits needed to lead the post Covid church?"

By far, the most cited trait was *flexibility*, or something closely related. I agree. Flexibility is one of the primary traits needed in churches, and needs to be practiced by church leaders. I've noticed, however, this is one trait many churches struggle to practice. We often get stuck in our "tried and true" methods. Even when those methods are no longer effective, the church struggles to change them. It seems we get stuck thinking and believing that the method is the mission. We often forget why the church exists.

> *Here is what I tell you. You are Peter. On this rock I will build my church. The gates of hell will not be strong enough to destroy it. I will give you the keys to the kingdom of heaven. What you lock on earth will be locked in heaven. What you unlock on earth will be unlocked in heaven.*

Matthew 16:18-19 (NIrV)

> *Jesus, undeterred, went right ahead and gave his charge: 'God authorized and commanded me to commission you: Go out and train everyone you meet, far and near, in this way of life, marking them by baptism in the threefold name: Father, Son, and Holy Spirit. Then instruct them in the practice of all I have commanded you. I'll be with you as you do this, day after day after day, right up to the end of the age.'*

Matthew 28:18-20 (MSG)

These two scriptures in Matthew are foundational to the church and its leaders. In the passage from Matthew 16, Jesus tells his disciples He will build the church. We, as followers, are not called to build the church. Jesus has got that part! In the Matthew 28 scripture above, Jesus tells us, His disciples, what our part in this is. Jesus tells us we are to go out and train everyone in His way of life. Too often we get stuck in thinking we are to build the church, when in fact, we are commanded to go out and reach new people with the good news of Jesus, training them in His ways. We are called to make disciples, not build the church (literally and metaphorically).

The pandemic has reminded (or maybe unfortunately taught) congregations that the building is not the church. There is no building required to be the church. The church is the congregation. The church is the people. The church is meant to be a movement of people sharing Jesus. The church is meant to teach and model the life of being a Jesus follower.

In *Fresh Expressions of People Over Property*, authors Warren & Carter offer this insight:

> Our church buildings, synagogues, and other religious places – which once stood as beacons of hope and reverence for its community – have become a burden for the organizations who seek to keep them standing. In efforts to patch leaky roofs and paint over years of wear, leaders are putting more and more money each year into property instead of people. The practices we have fallen into to keep a building running are not only demoralizing to the pastoral profession and the mission of the church, but they also run the risk of violating property tax laws and incurring more debt. What if our properties didn't have to be a source of pain but one of purpose and profit? [3]

We must become flexible in the ways we offer Jesus – in the ways we go and make disciples. At the same time, we cannot lose sight of our purpose – our mission. To be a healthy, vital, and culturally competent church in the post-pandemic world, we MUST become and remain flexible and

---

[3] Warren, Audrey and Kenneth Carter, *Fresh Expressions of People Over Property*, Abingdon Press. Nashville. 2020.

lose our tendency to be rigid and stagnate. When a person becomes sedentary and does not move, s/he loses muscle tone, bone mass, blood volume, and endurance. You have heard the old cliché, "Move it or lose it." The same is true for the church and its leaders. If we are not continuously practicing being flexible and constantly evaluating and adapting, we will lose the ability to do so.

What does it mean to be a flexible church with flexible leadership? According to dictionary.com, being flexible means:

Bending without breaking, able to be easily modified to respond to altered circumstances or conditions, or ready and able to change so as to adapt to different circumstances.

Common synonyms are:

- pliable
- supple
- adaptable
- adjustable
- open
- accommodating

When is the last time you have heard a church described with any of these adjectives? It's probably been a while, if ever. The church has found itself far from being flexible as a leading trait and practice. Yet, if we are to reach new, younger, and more diverse people in the post-pandemic world, we must become flexible.

> *"Adaptability comes from the integrity of character, values, identity, and serves as an unchanging leverage point for agile, innovative solutions."*
>
> **Tempered Resilience, Tod Bolsinger [4]**

Worship Flexibility

We need to be more flexible with worship options. In my work with hundreds of churches across the country, worship wars are some of the most common conflicts churches encounter. Some like one worship style. Others like a different worship style. Some like one genre of music. Others prefer a different genre.

I once worked with a church that decided to launch a new worship experience. They conducted a survey to inquire what kind of experience people desired. And who did they survey? I bet you already know the answer. They surveyed the people already attending the church.

How are we to reach new people when we are focused on appeasing the ones already a part of the church? A flexible church would be researching what the demographics in their community might like or asking what worship experiences would be welcomed. (FYI: MissionInsite offers this information.) This research would lead to the formation of new worship experiences that would be further shaped by first building relationships with the very people we are trying to reach.

Worship is to glorify God! Worship creates opportunities

---

[4] Tod Bolsinger, *Tempered Resilience,* IVP, 2020.

for people to encounter God through music, scripture, sermons, prayers, symbols, communion, etc. Different people encounter God in different ways on different days. When we become stuck in offering worship the same each and every Sunday, we are missing the opportunity for people to be moved by the Holy Spirit in different ways for new and different ears and eyes.

For guests or seekers, sometimes worship offerings feel as though they are encountering a foreign language. Worship offerings need to be relevant and offered in a "language" that is familiar and comfortable to seekers. When we become mired in a comfortable, preferred worship style, we have lost focus of our purpose.

Other common conflicts around worship changes include how announcements are handled, the meet and greet, children's time, and technology. When it is suggested that announcements could be offered on screens ahead of time or only in the bulletin, there is often push-back. This is true even when the announcements run way too long or include every ministry and activity. If announcements must be made, there should only be one or two and should apply to everyone in attendance.

The meet and greet is often uncomfortable for guests, goes on too long, and some people are ignored. In the post-pandemic world, I believe there will be even greater push-back and meet and greets should likely be eliminated. Children's time is often more for the adults. The adults like to see children march down the aisle and sit on the chancel steps at the front of the church. It is a feel-good moment. Yet, the effectiveness of the children's message, along with the safety of children moving from the sanctuary to a different part of the building for children's ministry, is questionable in today's world – and likely not seeker friendly.

Technology is another hot button for churches when it comes to worship. Let's be frank. The rest of the world communicates through technology. It is a common mode of communication. Technology allows so much more creativity and options for offering worship elements. The church must embrace technology.

For me, this is a non-negotiable. Not having technology in the church is like special ordering a brand-new car without air conditioning. Why would anyone consider this (unless you live in a cold climate and the car normally comes off the assembly line without air conditioning)? Check out *Building Worship Bridges*[5] for assistance on re-thinking worship and worship design.

The post-pandemic church must be a digital church. Whether this is a both/and approach (on-site and online) or only online, we must be a digital church. We must offer online ministry, not just online worship. Most of the people we are trying to reach are online. When we offer a pre-recorded worship service without offering relationship opportunities and next steps (i.e. discipleship, service, small group), we are not offering the full expression of the church.

There are several other ways churches lose their

---

[5] Townley, Kotan, Farr, *Building Worship Bridges: Accelerating neighborhood connections through worship*, Market Square Books, 2017.

flexibility around worship, but you get the idea. Worship must be relatable, contextual, relevant, and seeker friendly. We must remain flexible in the methods of worship while remaining focused on the mission.

Flexibility in Ministries

Everything has a life-cycle – including ministries. Everything has an expiration date – including ministries. Too often, the purpose and intended outcome are no longer in play, but a ministry, program, or event continues for years or decades.

- We simply do it because we have always done it.

- We continue to do it because we do not want to offend the person who created or led the ministry.

- We continue to do it because we would have no idea what to do instead.

- We continue to do it because we like to do it.

- We continue to do it because that is our understanding of what the church is "supposed" to do.

All these are great reasons, but they are not missionally based reasons.

The church offers ministries to help people take their first or next faithful step in discipleship for becoming a disciple-making disciple. Too often, a church blindly transfers this year's programs and events over to next year's calendar without any intentional evaluation or planning.

- What was the purpose of the ministry and its intended outcome?

- Did it meet the purpose and outcome?

- How are people growing in their faith as a result? How does this ministry help the church live out its vision and mission?

Post-pandemic churches must be flexible and adaptable in the ministries offered. We often burn out volunteers by having too many activities, yet we rarely stop to evaluate the effectiveness of all that busy-ness and usage of the most precious church resources – time and energy of the people in the congregation. Volunteer burnout results. Volunteers become frustrated in putting in so much time and energy without an impactful outcome or enough adequate help to carry out the ministry.

Often churches try to be all things to all people, thinking this shotgun type of approach will reach and connect with more people. However, the opposite is true. Having a defined niche, offering ministries targeted to this niche, and going deeper relationally has a much higher ROI (return on investment) when it comes to the energy and time of volunteers and missional effectiveness

Ministries are not a means to the end. The church does not exist to just keep busy doing ministry. We engage in ministry to live out our discipleship and introduce others to Jesus. Therefore, we must remain flexible and adaptable in the type of ministries, programs, and events we offer. If it is not helping people grow more Christ-like, or reaching new people for Christ, then we consider stopping the ministry. Post-pandemic churches need to strategically and intentionally offer only ministries that connect with seekers and help the congregation take their next faithful step in discipleship and become disciple-making disciples.

Flexibility in the Definition of Church

Church is no longer a date, time, and place with a program. In fact, it was never intended to be that. Yet, that is indeed what some churches have become and what many insiders still expect it to be.

The founder of Methodism, John Wesley, intended Methodism to be a movement, not an institution. Unfortunately, we have become a big, antiquated, dysfunctional institution. Not intentionally, but the result of not practicing flexibility (along with some other key traits offered in this resource), has resulted in us becoming settlers, rather than pioneers. That does not mean the local church has to fall into (or stay in) this trap. The local church is still by far the best, most logical, and most practical way to spread the Good News of Jesus Christ – regardless of the institutional condition. The local church can be the boots on the ground, people of faith doing life in community, and relational opportunities to fulfill the Great Commission.

To recapture the roots of being a movement, the church must rethink the definition of what it means to be the church. Jesus did not spend his time building and maintaining facilities and creating programs for people to come to Him and attend. Instead, Jesus was out amongst the people. He walked and talked with them. He dined with them in their homes. He listened to their stories. He joined them in community events and festivities.

In consulting with hundreds of churches and thousands of leaders across the country, it is heart-breaking to see how minute the portion of church budgets that actually fund ministry are. I typically see congregations spending about five percent or less of the budget on actual ministry. Most of the church budget is spent on facilities, utilities, insurance, staff, benefits, equipment, and supplies. I've seen churches with huge budgets allocate as little as $500 for children's ministry, and nothing for evangelism. Then, these same churches wonder why they don't have young families involved.

The church will have to be much leaner in the future

We need to find ways to operate with less overhead, allowing a much higher percentage of giving for actual ministry. We will also need to find creative and alternative methods to fund ministry beyond the offering plate. Check out resources like, *The Coming Revolution in Church Economics: Why Tithes and Offerings Are No Longer Enough, and What You Can Do about It,*[6] by Mark DeYmaz and Harry Li to dive deeper into alternative ministry funding.

---

[6] Mark DeYmaz and Harry Li, *The Coming Revolution in Church Economics: Why Tithes and Offerings are no Longer Enough, and What You Can Do About it,* Baker Books, 2019.

The post-pandemic church leaders must spend time in prayer and discernment. In your local context, what does it mean to be the church? What are the non-negotiables that must be present to "be" the church? Too often we find ourselves stuck in thinking there is only one way to operate, or only one exact truth or experience.

For example, one might think a requirement to be the Fourth of July is arriving at 4:00 pm sharp at Aunt Sally's house, where we grill pork chops, eat Grandma's potato salad, indulge in Uncle Bill's cherry cobbler with homemade ice cream, and enjoy the over-the-top fireworks display offered by crazy "pyrotec" cousin Larry. If any one of those elements is missing, then the Fourth of July is ruined. It just can't be the Fourth of July without Grandma's (secret recipe) potato salad.

In comparison, some would say it just wouldn't be the church without:

- the traditional worship with the same 50-year-old worship order in the church sanctuary

- a 10:00 am start time on Sunday morning

- the organ and choir

- monthly communion on the first (not the second or third) Sunday of the month

I'm guessing you get the point. In this example, the methods of how worship is conducted has become sacred, often believed to be the one and only way of offering worship. I do not remember Jesus declaring there is only one worship

34

order, or the first Sunday is *always* communion Sunday.

Sacred is holy and connected to God. There are many paths and methods for connection to God. Not just one. There isn't only one certain place. There isn't only one certain time. There isn't only one certain day. There isn't only one certain order. There isn't only one type of music.

To be a vital church in the post-pandemic world, we must break all the chains that we have placed on ourselves, chains that define what it means to be the church. Leaders who lead the church of the future will not be bound by methods, times, places, or programs. Bold leaders will be flexible and open to a variety of ways to be the church, while holding the essentials in place.

Flexibility in Leadership

To be the vital, healthy post-pandemic church, we will need to reconsider the type of leader it will take to lead the church for this new time. Leaders (both clergy and laity) will need to be more agile in thinking and doing. Leaders will be cheerleaders and advocates for change, rather than resistant and defiant. The leaders of the future church will embrace adaptability and be energized by innovation. Curiosity will be a driver in becoming and staying relevant. The leader will have both open hearts and open ears for people inside and outside the church, with a priority for the seekers.

Instead of being hypocritical – a common criticism of the church by outsiders – leaders of the post-pandemic church need to be bold and courageous. They will need to be vulnerable, because people are looking for leaders who are raw, real, and vulnerable. This means we share not only the favorable stories, but we are also vulnerable enough to share our own stories of failure, struggle, and despair. In other words, people are looking to connect with "real" people, not people that look like they have it all together, feeling the need to portray themselves this way, whether it's true or not. Leaders need to be self aware and willing to admit they don't know or were wrong. Leaders will lead with humility and determination.

The church may also need to be more flexible in what they look for in leaders. We have often been trained to place leaders on church boards or councils that have a specific experience or skill set (i.e., finance, accounting, human resources, building trades, real estate, etc.) as the primary qualification. Frequently overlooked is the need for mature disciples, living out their discipleship day in and day out. When immature disciples are leading the church, the leaders are leading with a secular lens, rather than a lens missionally-focused. This old style of leadership has resulted in churches managing people and assets in silos without accountability for being a disciple-making movement.

The Story

Recently, I was working with a church leadership team in the Northeast region of the U.S. We were engaged in strategic ministry planning. The church was in decline and the leaders were tired, weary, and nearing burnout. The average age of the leadership team and the congregation was around 70.

Part of the work of strategic planning is to look at community demographics. This particular leadership team had identified the scope of their mission field and we were reviewing demographics. One community demographic matched the existing congregation's demographic. Another growing community demographic related to the aspiring younger population. This group was missing from the congregation and had been for some time. As we looked at the types of leadership, facilities, small groups, service opportunities, worship, and hospitality the two different demographics desired, it became clear that this small church would not have the capacity to reach both population groups. These two demographics were polar opposites in what type of faith community experiences they desired.

Once the leadership team came to this realization, it first helped them understand why they were having trouble reaching this aspiring young demographic. Secondly, the leadership team knew they had a dilemma before them. Although some more intentional strategies would be needed, they felt they could likely reach some new people in the shared demographic. They wanted younger, more diverse people in their church, too. They shared their concern and reality that without younger people, the church would eventually die off. Yet, knowing what this younger demographic would be looking for, they knew they would not be comfortable being a part of this type of faith community.

They found themselves at a crossroads. They were struggling with targeting the people like themselves versus targeting the people who would be the future church. They felt they were in an "either/or" situation. Prompted by the Holy Spirit, I asked permission to offer a third option for their consideration. They readily accepted.

What if, rather than "either/or" we have a "both/and" opportunity before us? Puzzled by my question since we had just talked about the limited capacity of doing both, they asked me to explain. I proceeded. What if you were to adopt the strategies needed to reach your own demographic and you invest part of the principle of your endowment to hire a church planter to reach the aspiring young demographic and plant a new faith community as a part of your church? It would be a church plant within an existing church. I laid it at their feet for consideration, fell silent, and waited...

Several moments passed while the leaders absorbed the option and began to process and consider. One of the leaders reflected on how the primary donor to the endowment might feel about the question before them. She went on to say that she thought the donor would be very supportive of financially contributing to this forward-thinking ministry.

After a short ten-minute conversation, this leadership team called for a vote. This brave team unanimously voted to pursue planting a church within their church. When they were at the crossroads of either/or, they pivoted to both/

and. Rather than continuing to use the earnings of the endowment to cover some of the general operating costs, they took a faithful step to dip into the principle to invest in the future of the church. This leadership team realized both their limited capacity, but also the potential available to still be missionally focused because of the blessing of the endowment. They were willing to risk for the sake of the Kingdom. They were bold and flexible leaders who took the opportunity at hand and said "yes" to God.

Were they scared? Of course.

Were they excited? You bet!

Did they know exactly what the pathway ahead of them might be? No way!

Still, they stepped out in faith.

I have had the responsibility and opportunity to stand in that type of a moment with churches on several occasions. It is a humbling (and sometimes scary) experience to say the least. You are never quite sure how it will turn out. Leadership teams have the opportunity to make a big leap of faith, to be a new kind of flexible, to knowingly walk into liminality, or to walk away and play it safe.

On this particular occasion, I was not only humbled, but I was awe-struck by the unselfish, courageous act of faith these leaders took that night. This team felt it was the right thing to do and was surprised when I went on about how brave they were. This team didn't know was how many times I have witnessed leaders retreating, taking the easy way out, the path of least resistance. I have witnessed leaders becoming angry, taking their anger out on me for their current reality since I had been the one who named it. I've seen congregations decide to use their endowment to keep the lights on, a pastor in the pulpit, and the church open only to bury them, letting the next generation deal with the problem.

Unlike that church, this leadership team didn't realize is they were mature disciples of Jesus Christ who had a Kingdom perspective calling them to be flexible and adaptive for the sake of the gospel.

And they faithfully answered the call.

Bottom Line

We can't be the church of the future if we do not embrace and practice on-going flexibility. Flexibility allows us to adapt and respond quickly.

Unpredictability and change are modern day constants. If the church is to become and stay relevant, so we can live out the God-given mission, flexibility is not a "nice to have" practice, but a required trait and practice for the post-pandemic church and its leaders. We could learn from the Jesuits who live "with one foot raised" meaning they are always ready to respond at a moment's notice for making a difference in the world.

Questions to Ponder

1. How long has it been since worship has been evaluated? Is the current worship experience reaching new people? How open are you, the leaders, the pastor, and the congregation to changing anything in worship if it meant reaching new people?

2. What is the driving factor to determine what ministries are offered? How effective are the current ministry offerings in helping people take their next faithful step in discipleship and become discipling disciples? How effective are the ministries in reaching new people?

3. How would you define church? How would the congregation define church? What are the non-negotiables in your context for being the church? What is the underpinning for these non-negotiables?

4. How are leaders developed in your congregation? What kind of leadership traits are valued currently? Are these the same leadership traits that will help your leaders lead the future church? Why or why not?

Flexibility Assessment

Consider your current leadership and current church culture, how would you rate the practice of flexibility? Circle the number below that best represents its levels and practice of flexibility.

0=No Practice of Flexibility

10= Practice of High Flexibility

CHAPTER FOUR

Relational

*God is inviting us to journey to the land that God will
show us! As the Church of Jesus Christ, this invitation is a
powerful opportunity! The Church has talked about trying
new things, about being creative, adaptable, innovative,
nimble, and flexible and we have become more of these
things in this pandemic because we have had to. In this there
is hope. We can move outside our walls. We can cultivate
more connections and we can build more partnerships with
and within the communities we seek to reach for Christ. We
must recognize that the entry point for fulfilling our mission
is truly going where people are, beginning with the questions
they have and the challenges they are facing, instead of
expecting the people to come to us. This is a corrective call
for the church. Amid the pandemic we have rediscovered the
importance and need for the connections and relationships
that are not only possible but are happening in real time and
being birthed in new ways.*

Bishop Sandra Steiner Ball
West Virginia Conference UMC

The effective post-pandemic church will need to be
highly relational. Most churches would probably consider
themselves to be relational. In my experience, they would
actually refer to themselves as "friendly," and for the most
part, that would be true. They are indeed friendly, but most
often that friendliness shows up only with one another,
those already a part of the congregation, small group or

Sunday school class. In order to be relational, we have to think beyond being friendly with one another and move to being friendly with our community. We have to move onto building relationships in our community with those outside our current congregation.

To do this, the first step is to know our community. Part of getting to know the community is studying demographic information. I am certainly a big fan of this. However, we must move beyond learning about demographics to caring for, and investing in people. There are several shifts that will need to occur for us to become the highly relational church that will more likely reach new people in the post-pandemic world:

1. Shift from majority of energy and resources used on already gathered faith community to using energy and resources on those yet to be gathered

2. Shift from fear or denial of our mission to be in relationship with our neighbors to love, compassion, and empathy for our neighbors

3. Shift from driving into our church (often from a different part of town) on Sunday to being and living as part of the community surrounding the church facility seven days a week

4. Shift from attractional (expecting the community to show up at the building on Sunday) to dispatched movement (disciples sent to share the Good News)

5. Shift from program-driven to more intimate "doing life together" ministries

6. Shift from judgmental to "open ears" and "open hearts"

7. Shift from mono-cultural to multicultural and multi-generational

8. Shift from pastor-expected to disciple-responsible relationships

9. Shift from church-centric to community-centric

10. Shift from curriculum-driven to intentional discipleship pathway

11. Shift from self-guided to intentional, relational connections

12. Shift from building-driven to relationally-driven for both in person and online ministries

13. Shift from Sunday perfect to authentic: raw, real, honest, and vulnerable

14. Shift from top-down to alongside, two-way mentoring and discipling

15. Shift from insular to culturally competent and curious

Let's spend some time unpacking these shifts to gain clarity on what will be needed for these relational shifts to occur.

Shift 1 – Investing resources outside our gathered community

Think about the percentage of time (staff and congregation), building usage, budget, attention, and energy that is spent on the people who are already gathered as part of the church community. If you're like many congregations I've worked with, my guess is that 90 percent or more of your resources are used on the current congregation, leaving less than 10 percent (typically I see

3-5%) of our resources being invested in our neighbors yet to be gathered/reached for Christ. Think of what could be possible if we were to invest the majority of our resources in reaching new people! After all, isn't that what discipleship and being the church is all about anyway? Think of it as moving away from being the country club that has benefits and privileges for its members, instead moving into a deployment station to serve and share Jesus with others.

Shift 2 – Love, compassion, and empathy for our neighbors

To love our neighbors and demonstrate compassion and empathy would mean that we would have to first be in relationship with our neighbors (around the church and around your home). How are we intentionally investing in building relationships with our neighbors so that we can hear their stories, understand their fears and needs, and doing life alongside them? This is beyond providing a food pantry and collecting mittens. This is about investing in people – eyeball to eyeball, heart to heart.

Shift 3 – Doing life in the mission field

In the typical American church (particularly urban and suburban), many church attenders used to live in the neighborhoods surrounding the church. But over time, they have moved further out to newer,bigger homes, better schools, etc. Therefore, those attending the church for an hour or two on Sunday no longer have any connection (and thus no understanding of current reality) to the neighborhood. The post-pandemic church will be a church that is deeply and relationally connected to its neighbors. This is done best by living in the neighborhood and investing in it once again, experiencing life with the neighbors. This likely creates the need for a shift in how the pastor, staff, and key leaders think about their usage of time.

How much time is spent in the community each week? If the pastor is not spending a day or more per week in the community – meeting people – a shift in priorities is needed. If you have children, youth, and/or family ministries staff persons, they need to be spending time where kids and their families are hanging out: at ball games, schools, band concerts, the community swimming pool, etc. To do life in the mission field, we have to get away from expecting staff to be in the church building. The people we are trying to reach are not in the building, and the days of expecting the neighbors to come to us are over (and frankly have been for a long time).

Shift 4 – Becoming a sent and equipped movement

For many decades the church was the benefactor of being a cultural phenomenon. The culture used to be church-centric and people were attracted to the church as part of a cultural norm. Society basically shut down on Sunday to allow and respect this cultural norm. Over time, culture has shifted away from being church-centric. The church is now counter-cultural. Most people don't affiliate with a faith community. The post-pandemic church must finally rid ourselves of the notion that we can still rely on the attractional church model to prevail. Those days are over and have been for many years. We must restore our Wesleyan roots and once again become a movement, rather than having the settler attitude we have developed over time. The church is to equip and send people. We are to train disciples and send them out to reach new disciples.

Shift 5 – Relationally driven

Similar to Shift 3 – doing life in the mission field – we see being a disciple, a follower of Christ, as an honor and responsibility. We follow Jesus' lead and walk alongside people in life. Jesus didn't stay in the Temple and create the perfect curriculum for people to come and attend. Instead, Jesus was out and about among the people, walking alongside them in life, teaching, mentoring, telling stories and listening to stories. Effective post-pandemic churches will realize the perfect program or ministry offering is not a magic bullet. Instead, fruitful faith communities (all disciples, not just the pastor or the evangelism committee) will invest in people who do not yet have a relationship with Jesus. Being a disciple maker is relational. It is personal. It is what Jesus commissioned each of us to do.

Shift 6 – Open hearts, eyes, ears, and minds

One of the primary reasons most people of the Generations Y & Z want nothing to do with the church is because they deem the church to be judgmental and hypocritical. Unfortunately, they are often right. If we are going to become disciple makers, we will need to open up our hearts, minds, eyes, and ears in new ways. We will need to ask more questions, and show up with a sense of authentic curiosity for people and their story. We need to be willing to be transparent and real. We don't need to pretend we have it all figured out. We are going on to perfection, but we certainly have a long road ahead of us.

Shift 7 – Multi

Many of our churches are mono-cultural (i.e., middle class white folks with an average age of about 65). The typical congregation member looks, thinks, acts, spends, believes, and does life pretty similarly to other members. In contrast, this is not an accurate reflection of culture especially in larger communities. Paul Nixon wrote a book I highly recommend called *Multi*. In this book, he shared how churches will need to think about being multi in many different facets: Multi: cultural, ethnic, site, lingual, narrative, liturgical, theological, generational, and economic. A vital post-pandemic church will be a reflection of their mission field.

Shift 8 – Disciples as Disciple Makers

In many cases, churches have come to expect pastors (and sometimes staff too) to do it all and when it comes to ministry. We have become a pastor-centered church. The more denominations expected pastors to be professionally trained – navigating a tangled sea of the hoops for ordination, the more congregations became pastor-dependent and pastor-driven. Laity no longer felt equipped

49

for ministry. As a result, we are no longer a laity-led movement with an occasional circuit rider preacher, but instead have become pastor-centric. If your church finds itself in this place, check out the book, *IMPACT! Reclaiming the Call of Lay Ministry*.[7] Vital post-pandemic churches will shift the role of ministry from pastor expected to disciple expected. Mature disciples see ministry as their honor, privilege, and responsibility.

Shift 9 – Community Centric

Rather than thinking the community should have a heart for the church, a vital post-pandemic church will instead see the church as part of the community – a vital thread in the patchwork quilt of the town. Most often a church that closes its doors has become invisible to the community long before it actually closes. The church was no longer woven into the community or a vital part of the heartbeat of the community and therefore the church was no longer relevant or needed in the community. Fruitful and effective churches become a part of the center of the community rather than expecting the community to become church-centric.

Shift 10 – Intentional Faith Development

Many churches have gotten into the routine of seeing discipleship as something we learn – discipleship means head knowledge. Yet in his fullest expression, discipleship is growing more Christ-like in our doing, saying, being,

---

[7]   Blake Bradford and Kay Kotan, *Impact! Reclaiming the Call of Lay Ministry,* Market Square Books, 2018.

thinking, and becoming. When we limit discipleship to whatever the latest curriculum is, we have limited both the understanding and the development of being a disciple. Since the church is in the disciple making business, we need to have a pathway for people to engage with and become fully devoted followers of Jesus Christ who in turn disciple others. Without an intentional discipleship pathway in place, it is impossible for churches to raise up disciples consistently, effectively, and thoroughly. Vital, post-pandemic churches have an intentional pathway with multiple entry points and an expectation for faith development.

Shift 11 – Connectional and Relational

In working with hundreds of mystery worshipers and through my own experiences, seekers and first-time guests are most often left to their own devices to connect into the life of the church. While many churches have some sort of hospitality practices, they lack intentional means to build authentic relationships and help connect people into the ministries, discipleship pathway, and the life of the congregation. There might be a form letter sent from the office with the pastor's name, but usually that is about as far as the follow up occurs for first-time guests. This type of follow up is a mechanical, process-related task. Having a connectional team that is invested and gifted in building relationships with new people is imperative. The connectional team is not only highly relational, but also has intentional steps and systems to make sure no one is lost in the cracks. Vital churches in the post-pandemic world help disciples with relational spiritual gifts engage in this ministry of building relationships and connecting people.

Shift 12 – It's not about the building

You have heard it a million times – the church is the congregation. The church is not the building. Yet, the building has become central to our identity. When we go to church, we typically refer to going to the building. Much of our budget is spent on building, maintaining, heating, cooling, and remodeling our buildings, fixtures, furnishings, and parking lots. Vital, effective, post-pandemic churches will use its resources to focus on being relationally driven – first by relating to the unchurched, then by those attending – rather than decisions being based on the maintenance and/or preservation of the facilities. This includes both online ministries as well as on-site ministries.

Shift 13 – Raw, real, honest, and transparent

In order for the church to reach the most unchurched age groups, we must become vulnerable as a congregation, as a church, and as individuals. We will not be given the honor or opportunity to interact and build relationships if we put on airs and facades. Those under age 40 are looking for leaders who are relational, transparent, and willing to be raw, real, and honest. Not only will they want these attributes to show up in one-on-one relationships, but they are looking for these traits in sermons, church structure, and leadership (clergy and laity). Vital churches in the post-pandemic world can identify and are willing to risk vulnerability to reach new, younger, and more diverse people and are more likely to invite these young people in leadership positions.

Shift 14 - Coming Alongside

At all levels of society, the top-down approach has become less effective and trusted. The era of big institutions and complex systems are giving way to smaller, more localized organizations. The generations who have recently joined the workforce and will be joining the workforce in the coming years have been educated with a teaming, collaborative approach to learning and decision making. Decisions made without accountability behind closed doors are no longer trusted, let alone desired. Instead, people are looking for opportunities to work alongside others. Younger generations also desire two-way mentoring opportunities where those with more life experience share their experiences. Simultaneously, this offers younger generations to share their experiences with those of older generations. Post-pandemic churches that will be vital and fruitful will offer opportunities for mentoring and collaboration in leadership, relationships, and discipleship.

Shift 15 - Culturally Competent

This last shift is somewhat a summary of the other 14 shifts. If the church is to become culturally competent, with a high EQ (emotional intelligence, or some are referring to it as emotional humility), all the other shifts will become intuitive. When a person or organization leads from a place of on-going growth, curiosity, self-awareness, and value in cultural competence and emotional intelligence, they are far more likely to be effective. Yet to do this, we must be more focused on others than ourselves – something the church has struggled with historically. Churches who will be fruitful and effective in the post-pandemic world will invest in the congregation – specifically the leaders – becoming culturally competent and emotionally intelligent.

The Story

In rural Missouri, there is a town of less than 2000 people where the local United Methodist Church averaged about 160 people in 2016. That is a pretty great market share for a church in the modern world. The reason this church was so strong was because they were relational – inside and outside the church. Although there were multiple churches in town, when anyone at the local schools were to refer to "the church," it was this congregation.

The church provided a clothing closet for the community and the school personnel were provided gift certificates to give out to children as needed. The church hosted events (along with preparing the meals and serving the meals), such as the back to school and teacher appreciation luncheons. Disciples would be table hosts and build relationships with the teachers and administrators. Counselors and principals knew they could call the church if they or a student needed anything. The family ministries coordinator, pastor, other staff, and congregational members spent time at the school volunteering to read to children, assisting teachers, etc. The church and school were strong community partners. Both of them were vital to the heartbeat of the community.

In another first-tier (cities and towns outside of central cities and inside the ring of developing suburbs and rural areas) area, a church made a huge pivotal decision to invest in the community and build relationships. They chose to invest in the nearby grade school. The "Back to School Bash" was created and hosted by the church for the school. Hundreds of families attended. The principal was present, as were the local police and fire departments. As relationships continued to grow between the school and the congregation, some disciples invested by becoming reading partners or volunteering to help teachers at the school. The congregation celebrated special occasions with the school staff by offering meals and relationships. The pastor even became the school crossing guard. In the span of less than two years, this church built a strong relational bond with their local school resulting in church growth and vitality.

Bottom Line

Being the church means being in the relationship-building business. If a church is to live out its purpose and potential, it must both value and invest in relationships inside and outside the congregation. This has to be done at all levels of the church, and can't be reliant on hiring clergy and staff to do this for the congregation. The congregation is part of the community and must be the primary relational investor. Why would the church even exist, if it is not willing to have an on-going commitment and value for investing in new and existing relationships?

Questions to Ponder

1. Review the identified shifts above in becoming a highly relational church. Which shifts has your church already fully made and implemented? How are those particular shifts bearing fruit already?

2. Which shifts need work?

3. Of the shifts needing work, what shifts would you identify as priority for implementing? What made you choose them?

4. How difficult will these shifts be for the congregation? How will you equip the congregation to make these shifts? What obstacles might be encountered during the implementation? How will those obstacles be overcome?

Relational Assessment

Consider your current leadership and current church culture, how would you rate the overall practice of being highly relational? Circle the number below that best represents your church's rating of being highly relational.

0=Not at All Relational Inside and Outside

10=Highly Relational Inside and Outside

CHAPTER FIVE

Vision

The church has forever changed because of COVID-19 and both clergy and laity have had to reinvent the way they do ministry because of the pandemic. Isaiah 43:19 says, "Look! I'm doing a new thing; now it sprouts up; don't you recognize it? I'm making a way in the desert, paths in the wilderness."

The current disruption is actually a gift that will lead churches into new possibilities for outreach and evangelism, thus transforming their communities and the world.

Bishop Laurie Haller
Iowa Conference UMC

Being the pre-pandemic church without vision guidance was like wandering in a dark, starless forest without a compass, flashlight, or sense of purpose. For all we know, we are circling the same trees repeatedly, yet still expecting to make progress and find our way out. In a post-pandemic church without vision, it will be like wandering around on the moon without a spacesuit, means of communication, or a rocket ship, but expecting to find our way back to Earth.

Where there is no vision, there is no hope.

George Washington Carver

Where there is no vision, the people will perish.

Proverbs 29:18

Vision provides us with a sense of who and how God is calling us into the future. Every church has the same purpose (aka mission) documented for us in Matthew 28:18-20. Jesus commissioned us, His followers, to do as authorized and commanded by God. The commission is very clear.

The NIrV version of this scripture says, "so you **must** go...". There is a sense of urgency in this Great Commission. Don't stay and wait for people to come to the church. Go. You must go! Teach them, instruct them in "this way of life" (MSG).

> *Jesus, undeterred, went right ahead and gave his charge: "'God authorized and commanded me to commission you: Go out and train everyone you meet, far and near, in this way of life, marking them by baptism in the threefold name: Father, Son, and Holy Spirit. Then instruct them in the practice of all I have commanded you. I'll be with you as you do this, day after day after day, right up to the end of the age."*

Matthew 28:18-20 (MSG)

Even with this very clear direction from Jesus, I am still perplexed by the number of faithful church members who do not know or understand the purpose of the church. This speaks to the lack of discipling by many of our churches across the past several decades. This lack of discipling and understanding the church purpose has certainly contributed to the decline of the church and its impact on culture. Obviously, this must be the starting point because vision is the unique way a particular church makes disciples. Without a clear purpose/mission, there simply isn't a unique way for a church to live out the mission stated in the vision.

Start with an understanding and acceptance of the mission. Then proceed with the vision discernment which will articulate God's preferred future for your church in the unique way your church will make disciples over the next couple of years.

Vision for the Church

When it comes to vision discernment, I firmly believe this is a congregationally-driven process and discernment. If the pastor does the visioning alone, it becomes the pastor's vision rather than a congregational vision. This is of particular importance for a United Methodist Church, where a pastor is appointed for one year at a time and the denomination averages a five-year or less appointment tenure.

Vision should not be based on one particular person's thoughts and prayers, but rather many elements and people should be involved in the process. All of these need to be taken into consideration when determining a vision:

- Current needs of the community
- Current passions of the leaders

- Current gifts of the congregation
- General demographics of the mission field
- Community leader interviews
- Unchurched neighbor interviews
- Attributes of the targeted Mosaic segment
- Most importantly, discernment of God's preferred future for the congregation

This information is typically collected by a team, then shared with the congregation as part of a visioning day. The process is bathed in prayer and discernment. The process is to help discern God's preferred future for the unique way the church will live out the discipling purpose. The visioning day will also include a mission field prayer walk, table conversations, and small group activities. The visioning day will conclude with several vision rough drafts that will be taken by the pastor to finalize through prayer and discernment. The vision will be blessed by the leadership team and then rolled out for the congregation through a sermon series.

Churches that will be vital, fruitful, and relevant in post-pandemic times are churches that will have a compelling vision driving the church through its discipling, ministries, leadership, and resource alignment. According to the Bullard Church Life Cycle, when vision is driving a church, the church is healthy and growing. In contrast when structure is driving the church, the church is in decline. This is yet another rationale for a church to have a compelling vision. This is especially true when the vision is driven by the purpose of making disciples – or to be even more distinct – driven by the purpose of making disciple-making disciples.

Vision is no longer for a five-to-ten-year period like it once was. With the rapidly changing culture, vision must be visited often, likely recasted every couple of years. Any time there is a shift in the needs of the community, the demographics in the mission field, the passions of the leaders, and/or the gifts of the congregation the vision must be recast. The pandemic has likely caused a shift in one or more areas and most churches will need to go through a new visioning process. If we don't stay on top of the vision for its relevance and momentum-driving capabilities, we will likely find ourselves on the downward side of the life cycle in a plateau (at best) or decline (at worst).

> *And a vision of what is not yet before us, but that we can see with eyes of faith, hope, and imagination - when captured and cast- creates the shared motivation for confronting resistance and continuing tenaciously toward the larger transformative goal.*
>
> **Tod Bolsinger**
> *Tempered Resilience*

While many churches and their leaders are reluctant or resistant to casting vision, those churches who embrace a vision will thrive in the post-pandemic world. In the process of visioning, the leaders mine for information, interpretation, and cultural trends which will help them better lead for they have a better, on-going, understanding of their community and are invested in the process. This leads them to be more invested in seeing the vision become reality. The process of visioning helps the leaders become more culturally competent, providing the opportunity to become and stay more relevant and compelling to the community.

Vision for the Community

A vital church in the post-pandemic world will have a desire to have a positive impact in the community. Not only will there be a desire, but there will be energy, resources and momentum for doing so. By having a positive impact on the community, we are making a difference in the lives of our neighbors.

> *If anyone boasts, "I love God," and goes right on hating his brother or sister, thinking nothing of it, he is a liar. If he won't love the person he can see, how can he love the God he can't see? The command we have from Christ is blunt: Loving God includes loving people. You've got to love both.*

I John 4:21

A growing urban church in St. Louis, launched in 2006, has a church vision that includes a community vision of impact. The Gathering was launched with a "deep desire to make a significant impact on our city." This vision still continues to drive the culture and ministries at The Gathering as a community partner. There are even special hashtag campaigns at The Gathering from time to time that include naming the city.

When a congregation has a heart for their community, there is a resulting positive reverberation. Remember, we don't have a heart for the community because it helps the church grow. We have a heart for the city because, as a community of faith, this is who we are called to be. We should be the example, a model, for loving your neighbor for the rest of the community, because this is what Jesus told us to do. When we are faithful to His teachings, the church will be fruitful.

In my work with mystery worshipers through Impressions Unlimited (ImpressionsUnlimited.org), we train churches on first knowing, then improving their NPS, Net Promoter Score. This evaluative process has become a standard used by business and organizations for determining how well they are serving and retaining new and existing customers/clients. This evaluative process is new to the church world, but is helpful to better understand first-time guests' experiences. Among many questions relating to their experience, the church can learn much about a person's likelihood in returning to the church, as well as the likelihood of their recommending the church, by asking two simple questions. Through these two questions, a Net Promoter Score is tabulated. If guests from the community are walking away from a church experience without the desire to return or recommend, the church obviously needs to know and try to rectify it. The church often fails to consider how its community reputation is affected by those "will not return or recommend" experiences.

Vital post-pandemic churches understand why community perceptions are important and work towards continuously monitoring and improving those community perceptions. This is done by living out our discipleship by loving our neighbors, and living out our mission by sharing our faith with new people.

Vision for the People

Vital churches have the desire for transformed lives. Lives are transformed through the works of the church. One of the ways lives, hearts, and souls are transformed is through worship messages nestled in themed worship experiences. Messages are an important part of the worship experience. Done well, the message can carry the vision of the church and of the community. Furthermore, it can also offer a relevant, passionate story of God's love and promise. Our world and country are in need of healing. Seekers crave encouraging words of hope, love, and peace. If the church can't offer a vision of a better life for ourselves and one another, then who can?

Seekers are looking for a message that will make them ponder. As a modern society, we have access to all the information one could ever need in the palm of our hands. By and large, people do not come to listen to a message or experience worship to gain more information. They are showing up with anticipation of some sort of shift. Some sort of comfort. Some sort of peace. Some sign of love. Some answers to questions. They may even anticipate encountering God.

Competent, compelling post-pandemic churches understand the power of a relevant theme in a worship experience that brings all the elements together, including the message, to cast a more hope-filled, peace-filled, and love-filled existence for the people they have the privilege with which to share. They understand both the responsibility and privilege that comes along with having a vision for a transformed people.

The Story

A few years ago, I was working with a church in an older part of their town. Those attending the church once lived nearby, but no longer lived in the neighborhood. Most drove into the church's neighborhood only on Sundays due to a connection to someone else attending the church (i.e., family member). The church had been in steady decline for quite some time and had come into a season of questioning whether they would be able to continue to support a full-time pastor. With this question on the table, the conversation turned to the congregation's desire and capacity to take some of the responsibilities currently left to the pastor if they were to move to a part time appointment. When the church leaders were asked about their practice and strategy for building relationships with the neighbors in the community surrounding the church, the room fell silent. Finally, one leader spoke up and shared that they weren't too sure it was safe to be out meeting people in the neighborhood.

Bingo! There it is. This is the underlying cause for the decline in the church. The congregation had become disconnected and fearful of the neighborhood surrounding the church – the mission field the church was responsible for reaching. The congregation no longer had a heart for its neighbors. In contrast, they were fearful of the neighbors.

In my humble opinion, a church was commissioned to its mission where it was planted. Regardless of the changes in the neighborhood, as long as that church continues to be in that location, they continue to have a responsibility for reaching the surrounding community. This is another reason why the church needs to be a reflection of the neighborhood, rather than being a fortress or museum for non-neighbor members to come visit once a week. The church no longer has a positive impact on the community or the people residing in the community. In fact, seeing unfamiliar people come and go, along with activities occurring without being invited, the neighborhood might even be resentful of the church.

When a congregation's heart no longer breaks because the neighbors don't know Jesus, the congregation is no longer taking the honor and responsibility placed in their hands by the generations of faithful members who likely sacrificed to build the church. The congregation is no longer serving the purpose for which it was intended – to reach new people for Jesus. When the congregation has walked away from their responsibility, they need to also walk away from the property – Jesus' property. The property should be placed in the hands of the people of the community through a new church plant, a church serving the neighborhood in need of larger or better facilities, etc. Those attending the church need to attend church in their own neighborhoods, where they can do life alongside members of the community and fulfill their responsibility as disciples to share the Good News with other people.

Bottom Line

The effective church in the post-pandemic world will be vision-inspired and vision-lead. The church will see the layers of this vision through the lens of the church, the community, and the people. With this layered, triple focus, the vital church will be relevant to the neighbors, demonstrate a heart for the community, and have a driving passion for the church's unique method of making disciples of Jesus Christ to transform the world.

Questions to Ponder

1. What is the current vision of the church? How is it providing momentum and energy for the congregation in its mission to make disciples?

2. How does your church love on its community? How is the church the example of loving your neighbor?

3. What is the community's perception of your church? What brings you to this conclusion? Is this what we "think" it is or is this what we "know" it is currently?

4. How does your church message and provide opportunities for individuals transforming lives through Jesus?

Vision Assessment

Consider your current leadership and current church culture, how would you rate the overall practice of being a visionary church? Circle the number below that best represents the church's practice and results of being a visionary church.

0=Not at All Visionary

10=Very Visionary

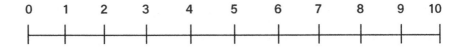

CHAPTER SIX

Spirituallly Grounded

*Effective leaders are attentive to the interior life,
strategic thinking and implementation.*

*All three are important because what we do and
how we do it flow from who we are.*

Bishop Debra Wallace-Padgett
North Alabama Conference UMC

*"I am the true vine, and my Father is the vineyard keeper. He
removes any of my branches that don't produce fruit, and he
trims any branch that produces fruit so that it will produce
even more fruit. You are already trimmed because of the word
I have spoken to you. Remain in me, and I will remain in you.
A branch can't produce fruit by itself, but must remain in the
vine. Likewise, you can't produce fruit unless you remain in me.
I am the vine; you are the branches. If you remain in me and I
in you, then you will produce much fruit. Without me, you can't
do anything. If you don't remain in me, you will be like a branch
that is thrown out and dries up. Those branches are gathered
up, thrown into a fire, and burned. If you remain in me and my
words remain in you, ask for whatever you want and it will be
done for you. My Father is glorified when you produce much
fruit and in this way prove that you are my disciples."*

John 15:1-8 (CEB)

The vital post-pandemic church will be led by leaders
who are spiritually grounded. Too often we see church

leaders, clergy and laity alike, who get so caught up in doing the work of the church that they lose connection with the "vine." The only time spent in the Word is while planning sermons or preparing for small group. Their spiritual life is dried up. Churches whose leaders are spiritually grounded "produce much fruit and prove that they are Jesus' disciples." It is simply difficult for a congregation to be led by leaders who are spiritually dried up.

Grounded in Prayer

Another characteristic of the church that will be fruitful post-pandemic, is it will be a praying church. The life and mission of the church is wrapped in prayer. The church believes and relies on the power of prayer. Prayer is the first step in any decision.

In her book *Open Road (from The Greatest Expedition series),*[8] Sue Nilson-Kibbey writes:

"You see, prayers asking for God's breakthroughs activate God's power and passion within each of us. Those who pray regularly for God's new possibilities and open doors find themselves habitually looking up and out with holy expectation. And as we set aside our own preferences in order to make room for God's, our hearts and minds then have space to discern and pursue God's next steps forward. In fact, God's future for us becomes irresistible."

I absolutely love this bold prayer! We are asking for God

---

[8] Sue Nilson-Kibbey, *Open Road,* The Greatest Expedition series, Market Square Publishing, 2021.

to lead us in new ways. We have no idea what that might be, but it is implied in this prayer that we will be bold and courageous in following God's lead, assured God will clear the path and guide us along the way.

Spiritual Depth

Congregations that are missionally focused are also spiritually grounded. They have intentional pathways for discipleship that not only encourage, but serve as the foundation of what the church does and offers. Since making disciple-making disciples is the purpose of the church, all the church connects people to discipleship. Sermons point people to the discipleship pathway. Ministries point, direct, and help people take their next step on the discipleship journey. Only mature disciples are called into leadership.

There is much more focus on discipleship than membership. Membership, when offered, is a step of commitment to growing as a disciple and an increased responsibility, not an elevation towards privilege, benefits, or graduation. Discipleship development is not just a nice thing to talk about or to offer, instead it is seen as an expectation of those involved in the life of the congregation – those that are followers of Jesus. The development is deeply based in growing more Christ-like and less about the latest curriculum or title. Discipleship is the on-going development of the whole being, not just increased knowledge of God.

Attention and intention of discipleship leads to maturing

disciples building a maturing congregation who, in turn, disciple others who mature into discipling disciples themselves. This is how vital churches grow their spiritual depth.

Results of Spiritual Depth

It is through this deep commitment to discipling that the congregation grows in their dependence on Christ. In developing a culture of being a praying church, a congregation discerns God's preferred future and next steps for the church rather than being reliant on having all the answers ourselves. There is freedom that comes from this along with being less anxious. Fear of the unknown is washed away with confidence in total reliance on God's faithfulness.

When mature, devoted disciples are being formed in the healthy and effective post-pandemic church, a natural result is humbleness. Mature disciples are humbled by how God led them in their discipleship pathway and carried them in the journey when they couldn't walk alone. Mature disciples are humbled by how God keeps showing up in both their personal lives and the life of the congregation, blessing both abundantly. Mature disciples continue to be in awe of the power of God, creation, and grace.

When the congregation has a significant population of mature disciples, the passion for Christ is undeniable. Disciples are more willing to serve. Disciples are more generous. Disciples are more committed. Disciples are more dependable. Disciples are bolder and more willing to take risks for the sake of the Kingdom. Because of their deep relationship with Christ, mature disciples can't help but be passionate about sharing Christ with others and making sure the church is doing all it can to spread the Good News. Mature disciples are passionate disciples. Passionate disciples are attractional disciples.

The Story

When you walked into the church facility, you could feel it. You couldn't name it per se, but you could feel something was awry. There was a feeling of heaviness, sadness, and despair. After working with the church for just a short time, I could finally name it. This church was not spiritually grounded. This church was engaged in deep conflict. The sides had been chosen and the heels were deeply dug in. It was heartbreaking. Over the course of the next year, the pastor and staff invested highly in discipleship and conflict management. The church became a praying church. The bullies finally realized they would not prevail and left. The congregation breathed a sigh of relief and regained the missional focus that had been lost in the conflict.

There was not only deep spiritual healing, but also deep spiritual development, all bathed in prayer. When I walked into the building, I could feel it. I could name it. It felt good – warm, joyful, and inviting. The Holy Spirit swept over me like a breath of fresh air. This was the house of the Lord, and the people were serving the Lord once again.

Bottom Line

To be a fruitful, vital post-pandemic church, we must be a spiritually-grounded faith community. We must be intentional and expectational in being discipled and discipling others. Leaders model this by spending time collectively and individually in prayer, reading scripture, and with God – connected to the vine-modeling spiritual groundedness for the rest of the congregation. All we do is grounded in prayer with a complete reliance on God as we do our part in furthering the Kingdom.

Questions to Ponder

1. What is your congregation's intentional pathway to disciple existing and new believers?

2. What percentage of your congregation is on an intentional pathway for discipleship development? What could be done to engage more in development?

3. How would you describe the vibrancy of your congregational prayer life? What brings you to this conclusion? How might it be improved?

4. How are current leaders chosen in your church? Are the most mature disciples leading, or do we have other criteria for leadership? If so, what and why?

Spiritual Groundedness Assessment

Consider your current leadership and church culture, how would you rate the overall level of the congregation's spiritual groundedness? Circle the number below that best represents your congregation's overall spiritual groundedness.

0=Not All At All Spiritually Grounded

10=Highly Spiritually Grounded

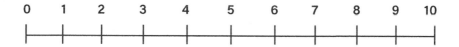

CHAPTER SEVEN

Commitment

"You always have two choices:
your commitment versus your fear."

Sammy Davis, Jr.

When we talk about commitment, we often think about commitments in relationships such as marriage. Perhaps we think about a commitment in terms of a legal commitment such as a mortgage, installment loan, or credit card, where we have signed a legally binding contract, promising to fulfill the terms and pay off the debt over a specific period of time. According to dictionary.com, commitment is defined as "the state or quality of being dedicated to a cause, activity, etc. or an engagement or obligation that restricts freedom of action." I am guessing that first definition was easy to hear, but the second definition might have taken you by surprise or perhaps even set you back a bit especially when we think about that definition of commitment as it relates to the church.

Commitment to Christ

In my work with churches across the country on church structure (how we organize ourselves to lead the church and make decisions), accountability goes hand-in-hand with structure. In the book, Mission Possible (co-authored with Blake Bradford), we hit hard on the need for accountability when it comes to leadership in the church. In the organizational model we recommend for United Methodist Churches:

- Staff and ministry team leaders report to the pastor
- The pastor reports to the leadership team
- The leadership board reports to Jesus Christ

Now let's take that model up a notch and look at it from an accountable leadership perspective:

- The staff and ministry teams leaders are held accountable by the pastor
- The pastor is held accountable by the leadership team
- The leadership team is accountable to Jesus Christ

Have we really thought about our accountability and therefore commitment to Christ and the Great Commission as a leader? As leaders of the church's board or council, we are accountable to Christ for leading the church in a way that fulfills the purpose. How many church board or council meetings have you attended when the ultimate question of accountability is asked? Leaders, how are we doing at leading the church in making disciples? How many new people in our mission field now have a relationship with Christ because of the ministry we are responsible for leading?

So often the church places people in leadership positions without training or expectations. Then we are disappointed that the church is not being more effective in reaching new people. Unless expectations are set differently, leaders will typically make decisions on what they personally believe is best and/or how the church has traditionally been led. This means if we don't have leaders who are devoted – mature disciples who understand and are committed to the church's purpose as Christ indicated – they will likely be unable to lead the church in alignment with this purpose and with accountability to Christ.

When was the last time your leaders asked one another at their regularly scheduled meetings how the church was doing at making disciples of Jesus Christ who are transforming the world? We must gain this type of clarity and commitment to be the vital post-pandemic church. This must become a non-negotiable standard of expectation for leaders – clergy and laity alike.

Commitment to the Church

In unpacking commitment to the church, let's first explore what it does not mean. Being committed to the church is not a commitment to:

- the building
- the 10 am Sunday morning service

- our fellow Sunday school friends
- the third Saturday of January chili supper
- the preschool/daycare
- the historic pipe organ

While all of these things are wonderful and have been a part of what we called church pre-pandemic, the post-pandemic commitment to the church must be different. Remember, those types of commitments were by and large ineffective pre-pandemic and won't be effective post-pandemic.

By having a commitment to the church, this means you personally and your congregation collectively believe that a faith community (local church) is the best means and mode to reach people for Christ. In the United Methodist Book of Discipline (2016) it states in ¶120:

> The mission of the Church is to make disciples of Jesus Christ for the transformation of the world. Local churches and extension ministries of the Church provide the most significant arenas through which disciple-making occurs.

In the latter part of ¶121 it further states:

> Wesley, Otterbein, Albright, and our other spiritual forebears understood this mission in this way. Whenever United Methodism has had a clear sense of mission, God has used our Church to save persons, heal relationships, transform social structures, and spread scriptural holiness, thereby changing the world. In order to be truly alive, we must embrace Jesus' mandate to love God and to love our neighbor and to make disciples of all peoples.

Church, do we hear this? Read it again. As the people

of the church and as disciples of Jesus Christ, there is an undeniable purpose for our existence as a church and the leaders leading the church. Did you notice these words specifically, "Whenever the United Methodism has had a clear sense of mission"? It is only when we had this clear sense of mission that God has been able to use the church to save, heal, transform, spread, and change! Our commitment to being the church that God can use is absolutely critical. This is a non-negotiable.

Commitment to the Community

By being committed to Christ first and to the church second, we naturally flow into a commitment to the community. This commitment to the community is two-fold. Our primary commitment is to those in the church's mission field who do not yet have a relationship with Christ. Our secondary commitment is to those who already have a relationship with Christ but need accountability to their continued commitment and growth as a disciple growing ever more mature and devoted to Jesus Christ as a part of our gathered faith community. It is important to understand and be fully committed to the priorities in this order. Too often our priorities are reversed. Furthermore, we end up using all of our resources (time, energy, budget) for those already gathered, leaving nothing for those not yet gathered. We must put these priorities in the proper order, and with proper focus.

This full priority commitment to the community must be about an introduction to Jesus, followed by discipleship.

In the post-pandemic world, it is not necessarily about getting them back to the building. This commitment to the community may look very different than what it has looked like in the past. It may be different kinds of gathering, different days than Sunday, micro-sized groups, different locations, online or in person, one-on-one mentoring, or different activities. If a person is growing in his/her relationship with Christ, we just can't be concerned about how it looks or comes to be. It is the outcome (growing disciples) that is important, not how (method) it is happening. This will be one of the hardest shifts to make for many. This is where we are of the culture and in the culture of our mission field. This is when we will be better able to reach new people and meet them right where they are, walking alongside them to help them to get to know Jesus. When we are in their element, they are likely more comfortable and we will have the best chance to make a connection. It's likely our commitment to the community might lead us to be uncomfortable. Hopefully this discomfort will be for only a short time, until being a part of the unchurched culture becomes the norm of a disciple-making disciple.

I think God is rejoicing when a family sits in their living room in their jammies having French toast while engaged in a new worship experience three states away, or when a group of men are hanging out in their canoes and tie up to one another's' canoes to pray together and talk about their week, or when five women who are struggling being wives, mothers, and/or corporate leaders gather for a virtual happy hour on Friday night after putting the kids to bed to offer support, encouragement, and look to scripture together for guidance.

The Story

There once was a church that had recently moved to a simplified, accountable structure (a streamlined form of congregational governance). This church had been dipping into endowments to meet regular budget needs for years. The budget had not been balanced for years. There appeared to be no deep concern for these practices when either the pastor or the consultant pointed out the issue to the leadership team. Through somewhat unrelated congregational training, a few folks outside the leadership team expressed concerns about the church's financial circumstances, as well as how other assets were not being leveraged for the church's mission. It was as though there was an awakening on the leadership team. It was as if they were hearing these concerns with new ears. There was a shift in awareness, energy, and momentum. At least that's what it looked like at the time, but the momentum was short-lived.

Once the leadership team was no longer hearing from anyone outside the leadership team, the awakening seemed to return to slumbering. The leadership slipped right back to their old way of thinking. The leaders were sure there would be another death that would take care of any financial shortfalls, unexpected expenses, and capital improvements that were never budgeted. That's how it had worked in the past. Why wouldn't it continue to work the same way in the future (even though the church was a third the size it was twenty years ago)? Furthermore, the leadership team blocked the pastor from making much needed staffing changes to better align to the mission and vision due to potential congregational push-back. Through their actions and inactions, the team seemingly cared more about community and congregational perceptions than the mission. What would the neighbors think if they knew the offering didn't cover the budget? What would the congregation say if this beloved (ineffective) staff member were released?

This church asked for a pastor to lead them out of their decline. Such a pastor was sent to them. The leadership team heavily invested in training and coaching. But when it came down to it, they just were not committed enough to the mission to make the needed changes. They were entangled relationally, which kept them fearful and blinded them to what could be possible if they led towards the mission instead. Their commitment was focused on avoiding conflict. Their commitment was to maintain internal (although unhealthy) relationships, rather than the mission. This "fairytale church" had all the resources (and more) than it could ever need or want to be vital and fruitful, but unfortunately the ending to their story was not, "and they lived happily ever after..."

> *"The only limit to your impact is your imagination and commitment."*
>
> **Anthony Robbins**

Bottom Line

The commitment we are called to is not just a word. It is a call to action. When the commitments to Christ, the church, and the community are made, and we hold one another accountable to these commitments, God will be able to better use us to be the church God desires. We can once again become the church that God created to save, heal, transform, spread, and change the world. It is only when we are committed to being the church as God imagined that the full power and possibility of the church will be realized.

Questions to Ponder

1. How is the purpose of the church continuously communicated and shared so it can be understood and embraced in your church?

2. How, when, and where is the accountability question of "How effective is the church in its fulfillment of the mission?"

3. What could be done to improve the accountability towards the mission fulfillment?

4. What are some shifts that would need to occur so the mission becomes the driving force – with investing in seekers – as a first priority?

Commitment Assessment

Consider your current leadership and church culture, how would you rate the overall level of the commitment to Christ, the church, and the community? Circle the number below that best represents the level of commitment to Christ, the church, AND the community.

0=No Commitment

10=Unquestionable Commitment

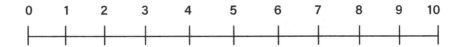

CHAPTER EIGHT

Innovative

As a church, we've never been this way before. The post-pandemic church will be different. It should be different for the outsiders and must be different for the insiders. It has to be different for the faithful. The pandemic mandates the church to be different, not to survive but to thrive for the sake of the gospel of Jesus Christ. Not shallow but profound self-innovation and transformation is the answer. The operative words for the post-pandemic church come from Jesus: "Put out into deep water, and let down the nets for a catch," Luke 5:4.

Bishop Jeremiah Park
Susquehanna Conference

Innovation no longer remains a choice but has become an imperative.

Narendra Modi

If the pandemic has taught us anything, I hope it has strengthened our willingness to experiment. As we all worked our way through the necessary changes allowing us to go about our personal lives in new ways during the pandemic, so did the church. Not all the things we tried first worked. Sometimes they failed. Failure is a teacher, not a destination or an ending. So often we get caught up in the fear of failure that we don't even try something new. This is often true for the church. We have to get over this. The urgency of sharing the gospel should help us remove, or overcome, our fears. "Fear not" is the most prevalent theme in the Bible, used an estimated 366 times. Fear not, experiment new ways to be the church in this post-pandemic world.

Most organizations budget for research and development (R&D) each year. The percentage of budget committed to R&D ranges from 0% (Chevron and Exxon) to nearly 45% (Celgene healthcare, craft.co, 2017 report) with a 10% average across several sectors. Furthermore, statistics would also correlate the amount spent on R&D is directly related to revenue growth. The more a company is committed to R&D, the higher likelihood of revenue growth.

"Innovation distinguishes between a leader and a follower."

Steve Jobs

What does organizational research and development have to do with the church? Simple answer: Everything. Like companies and other organizations, the church must continually innovate how we live out our mission of reaching those who do not yet know Jesus. Still, we often do not invest any of our resources to do so. In addition, we often don't encourage innovation as we find ourselves stuck in traditions that no longer serve the mission. Other times, we get trapped into thinking the church methods are sacred and therefore could not possibly be changed. We know that the mission doesn't change, but our methods must change. We've also found ourselves in an antiquated institution with outdated polity finding it difficult to adapt and streamline, causing us to be further mired down working in systems of the past rather than present or future.

The vital post-pandemic church will embrace innovation through multiple practices. One of those practices will be embracing innovation through investment in resources (dollars, people, energy). Another practice will be a spirit of experimentation without fear. These congregations will embrace the culture of a working lab – constantly researching, experimenting, testing, and developing new ideas and methods for being missionally effective in reaching people. New things will be tried and evaluated. When they work effectively, innovations are celebrated. When innovations do not work out, these churches continue evaluating, adapting – stopping when needed – and learning from the innovation experiment.

Methods will be seen as temporary, current ways of doing things. They won't be seen as the only way or as "the way." All the church does is based on living into its mission and vision. When it works, great! When it doesn't, they move on quickly and try something else. Innovation is part of the church culture in vital, healthy churches.

Rather than squelching creativity, vital healthy churches in the post-pandemic world will embrace and encourage creativity at ALL ages. Creativity is not seen as a threat towards tradition, but celebrated as potential new methods for being missional, for being faithful, and for being the church God has called us to be. Everyone is invited to participate, and inter-generational think-tanks are encouraged.

"Phygital" Church

Healthy post-pandemic churches will embrace online ministry. This means not just offering worship experiences, but offering a full expression of the church online.

Digital church is here to stay. It will not replace on-site worship and ministries, but a vital church understands it needs to be fully invested in the phygital world (physical and digital). The church was thrust into the online world due to the pandemic. While some churches were already invested in online ministry, others were partially online, while many churches went online for the first time. The pandemic thrust technology into the future for most churches overnight. Growing, healthy churches learned that this new digital method is able to reach people who might never be reached by on-site ministry. The churches that will be vital, healthy, and reaching new people in the post-pandemic world, will be the churches that embrace both on-site and online ministry.

It is important for the congregation and leadership to understand the "why" behind the decision to go online when the pandemic hit. If the decision was based only in providing a worship experience for the "regular" congregation, then the greater opportunity was lost. Churches that went online to provide for existing members only – not growing into the larger "why" of intentionally reaching new people –are likely to abandon online ministries once the facility reopens. This means an opportunity was missed. Innovation was knocking on the door, but not invited in. On the other hand, congregations that saw this opportunity, took advantage, and invested in innovations are the congregations that are reaching new people in new ways and discovering a changing landscape of ministry.

Vital churches have made staffing changes to accommodate this new phygital reality. These staffing changes include changes such as changing job descriptions, cutting some positions (i.e., staff unable to pivot, no longer have needed/required skill set, position eliminated), hiring new positions (i.e., online pastor and/or worship host, communication, technology), staff budget changes (i.e., decrease as percentage of the budget and/or higher percentage for online ministry), etc. While staffing changes (especially of long-tenured employees) are difficult, the vital church makes the changes for the sake of the mission, rather than being constrained by not taking the needed bold steps to release beloved employees.

Creating content and offering it online in a variety of ways and packages is what works for vital churches. People Google everything. When content is provided online, people are more likely to connect with it in the digital world than only a live on-site experience with limited attendance within a limited time frame. Innovation, creativity, and technology are used to offer and distribute content that helps unchurched people connect. Imagine someone going through a really difficult time in their marriage and they go online to search for help, answers, or hope. They find a podcast or article from the church that provides some assistance, hope, and a possible next step. Online content by and large is not expensive to create and can build up credibility over time through repeated views and opportunities to connect with the mission field. Having the right communication and technology strategies creates the opportunity for content to go viral. Keep in mind however, content can't be a standalone strategy for online ministry. Content may be the initial entry point, but ministry is about relationships. The church must be highly relational both online as well as in-person.

Innovative Strategies for Finances and People

Vital churches will likely find innovative ways to provide multiple revenue streams. These might include leveraging the facility and parking resources for income, creating separate 501(c)3 entities for other nonprofit funding and grants, creating separate for-profit entities, and other entrepreneurial ventures. These churches do not dilute or lose their mission in the midst of the other opportunities. Rather, these churches see using their assets as a leverage point so the mission can prevail. Again, check out Mark Deymaz's book, *Coming Revolution in Church Economics,* for some great insights and stories on how churches are creating multiple revenue streams beyond the offering plate.

Healthy churches also think about how to empower and embrace the sending of laity into ministry, becoming less clergy-dependent. In the United Methodist Church, clergy costs are extremely expensive when adding together compensation, pension, healthcare, housing, reimbursables, and continuing education dollars. Most churches are struggling to support one pastor let alone associate pastor(s). Vital churches are refocusing on equipping and sending laity into ministry to lead house churches, micro churches, missional communities, marketplace ministry, online churches, etc. Healthy churches do not do this simply because it is less expensive. Instead, they use this strategy because it is what was always intended, and more people can be reached through the 98% plus of the church's population that are laity rather than relying on the less than two percent of the clergy population to do so.

Another trend we are seeing in vital churches is bi-vocational pastors. This is not a strategy to have a pastor have a secular job until her/his church job becomes full-time. Rather, this is an intentional strategy to have workplace ministry/ministers. Imagine a church where multiple people have some theological training (probably not ordained) and are both an employee and the spiritual leader in a workplace or area of town. This is typically someone who is deeply connected and highly respected in the community with secular, vital job training. This position could even be part of an entrepreneurial social ministry with a separate income stream for the church. The idea is that this type of ministry strategy provides more relational boots on the ground for far less money than a typical clergy person.

Leadership That Embraces Innovation

Churches that will be competent, compelling, and missionally effective in the post-pandemic world will recruit, retain, train, deploy, and invest in quality leaders who thrive in an innovative culture. Innovative leaders attract other innovative leaders. If a church is not willing to risk and invest in innovation, they will likely not retain quality leaders who will be able to take the church very far in this post-pandemic world. Without innovation, most institutions won't survive long. At best, they will have a slow, painful death.

> *"Leadership should generate capacity, not dependency."*
> **Ronald Heifetz**

Vital churches embrace creative leaders who are honest. They speak the truth with love and grace even when the truth is difficult to speak and for leaders to hear. Likewise, the church appreciates and encourages truth-speaking leaders. These innovative leaders make themselves vulnerable by being willing to experiment knowing not all innovations will work. Innovative leaders often paint pictures of what can be and ask others to dream about what is possible by asking and encouraging lots of input, which leads to creativity. This allows multiple minds to massage an initial idea into an elevated idea.

> *"Effective leadership is not about making speeches or being liked; leadership is defined by results not attributes."*
> **Peter Drucker**

Churches who have a culture of innovation know that it does not necessarily take a large team to be missionally effective. They rely on the quality of innovative people, rather than quantity. A few of the right people will be much more effective than a large group of others to fit the innovative culture. Innovation is not only supported and encouraged, but it is also rewarded in vital churches. Great leaders often lead with great questions and do not feel the need to have all the answers. Great leaders leading highly effective and vital churches surround themselves with people who they invite, expecting them to challenge one another. The team can speak to the leader without fear of retaliation when the leader is wrong or other ideas need to be considered. Highly effective leaders are valued not only for what they speak, but are also highly valued for how they think. Strategic, innovative leaders are priceless.

The Story

A couple of years ago, I was introduced to a new church plant that was trying an innovative church planting strategy. This was not the typical standard strategy of building a launch team that would help build a faith community, eventually coming into a regular space for worship and ministry. Instead, the church planter had spent some time in the community getting to know people, the needs of the community, and identifying the community/ connectional gaps. The needs for both a community space to gather, along with the lack of a clothing consignment shop with affordable clothing, were identified. Based on those needs, the planter developed an entrepreneurial innovation strategy for ministry.

The planter partnered with a business that would provide space for a resale clothing shop at little to no cost to get started. The planter partnered with several churches to donate clothing for the shop inventory. The planter hired a Christian to be the cashier and provide customer service for its clients. The planter hosted multiple community conversations in the "conversation corner" of the shop on topics of high interest that he learned about during his time on the ground learning about the mission field. This served multiple purposes:

- It got people into the shop
- It showed both investment and great commitment to the well-being of the community.
- It allowed the planter to engage in conversation with new people
- It raised awareness of the business (opportunities to purchase, donate, and awareness the community space was available)
- It created a Christian shopping experience for the community

The planter also built relationships that lead to small groups being hosted in the shop as well as a small shop to premiere local arts, crafts, foods, etc. for local people. Eventually a worship opportunity was also launched in the resale shop once there was awareness and community.

Bottom Line

Innovation is key to the church who wants to be effective in fulfilling its mission in the post-pandemic world. This includes innovation as a value and culture, as well as investing and supporting innovative leaders. Innovative churches are not threatened by innovative leaders; these leaders are embraced. Without innovation, the church will simply not survive. Innovation is not about letting go of our Christian beliefs. It is about innovating how we share, communicate, and methodize those beliefs so the post-pandemic world can hear the message in a language and mode they can understand and embrace.

Questions to Ponder

1. Does your current church culture embrace innovation? What brings you to this conclusion?

2. What percentage of your current budget is devoted to R&D? How is this budget determined? Has it always been this percentage or amount?

3. How open do you believe the congregation might be to embracing a culture and practice of innovation to become more missionally effective?

4. What examples of innovation sparked your attention and why? What innovation could you imagine your church embracing in the upcoming months?

Innovation Assessment

Consider your current leadership and church culture, how would you rate the overall current level of the commitment to innovation? Circle the number below that best describes the current level of commitment and practice of innovation.

0=No commitment to Innovation

10=Fully Committed and Practicing Innovation

CHAPTER NINE

Resilience

Kathleen Norris in her book, Cloister Walk, got it correct when she wrote: "With God there is always more unfolding; that what we can glimpse of the divine is always exactly enough and never enough." This unfolding nature of God's will and mission is why we have the opportunity and the need to say "yes" every day. So we don't miss the important thing God, in Christ, is calling us to do.

Bishop Bruce R. Ough
Executive Secretary, Council of Bishops, The United Methodist Church

When I think of resilience, I often think about service men and women. These dedicated men and women get up each day – often away from their families – and continue to put one step in front of the other to serve and protect their beloved country. In the days of the pandemic, those serving in healthcare were certainly resilient. These dedicated women and men worked tirelessly and endlessly to treat and care for patients who are often alone and separated from their families. These healthcare workers put their own lives at risk to care for others in situations without always having the supplies, equipment, or adequate levels of personnel. Indeed, both our healthcare workers and our service women and men are heroes and outstanding examples of resiliency.

What does it mean to be a resilient church? Resilient churches are churches that do not allow setbacks to keep them down. Resilient churches are tough. They spring back. They get up and try again. Resilient churches may fall down, but they don't stay down. These vital churches are determined to be the church God is calling them to be and will not allow any circumstances or setbacks to keep them from this faithful journey.

Resilient churches are flexible. Remember, flexibility is the number one practice of vital churches in the post-pandemic world. Just like many of the other practices identified, resilience and flexibility go hand in hand. Remember that popular slogan, "Weebles wobble, but they don't fall down?" I believe this is perhaps another way to describe a resilient church.

> *I believe there exists throughout America today a rampant sabotaging of leaders who try to stand tall amid the raging anxiety-storms of our time . . . whenever a (group) is driven by anxiety, what will also always be present is a failure of nerve among its leaders.*
>
> **Edwin H Friedman**

Resilient churches are led by resilient leaders. Resilient leaders are ones that are positive, while also being realistic. They don't own rosy glasses, but when there is a will (and there is with these leaders), these resilient leaders will always find a way. Resilient leaders are those that are leading transformation. They are adaptive leaders who expect and embrace accountability. They don't focus on pacifying those already gathered. Instead they are missionally focused leaders who are vulnerable, self-aware, and humble The resilient leaders do not automatically respond with all the ways something won't work. Instead, resilient leaders instinctively and automatically respond from a place of immediately exploring ways that it can work. These leaders wholeheartedly believe in Albert Einstein's famous quote, "In every crisis lies opportunity." Not only do they believe in the spirit of this quote, but they act upon finding every possible opportunity when others might give up.

Along with being positive, resilient churches and their resilient leaders are also encouragers. Others in the congregation and the community are encouraged by their resiliency, hopefulness, tenacity, and positive attitude – all demonstrated in how these leaders go about leading in all aspects of their lives. These leaders are role models that others look up to and aspire to become. On the flip side, these leaders are also ones who offer encouragement verbally. They are the first ones to point out the win, what can be celebrated in the situation, the silver lining, progress that has been made, the effort invested, or the positive character traits used by the person involved. Whenever others encounter the encourager, they are lifted, inspired, and depart with more spring in their step. The encourager knows how to encourage, support, and even offer constructive criticism without tearing down another person.

Resilience is another reflection of strength. Those churches and leaders who exude resilience are often thought of as being strong leaders and congregations. They have strength that runs deeper and wider than most and seem to be able to pull out enough strength for any circumstance whenever needed. For me, strength is not a reference of muscle power, but it is a congregation or leader's ability to endure and persist in both the best and the worst of circumstances. Resilient leaders and resilient congregations find their power and strength in the Holy Spirit, where there is an unlimited supply no matter what the demand is.

> *The Lord is my strength and my shield.*
> *My heart trusts him.*
> *I was helped, my heart rejoiced,*
> *and I thank him with my song.*
>
> **Psalm 28:7 (CEB)**

Resilient congregations and leaders are not facing their first challenges or setbacks. Resilient leaders are resilient because they have faced challenges along the way and have built up their resiliency as a result. Some of the most resilient people I know have faced the greatest adversity! While they could have stayed down after the umpteenth time of falling, they instead chose to get back up time and again. And each time they got back up, they would rise with more strength and resilience than before. They have learned from those times of falling because they are self-reflective. The times of falling are not times of failure, but are times of learning and growing as a leader.

As a credentialed coach, I have had the honor and privilege of working with countless Christian leaders (clergy and laity) across the country. The most effective leaders are those who continue to invest in their development through on-going learning, coaching, spiritual direction, counseling, and peer mentoring. Those leaders who I have worked with see the value in coaching to work on personal foundations, leadership foundations, balcony views, and greater self awareness.

Because this is not the resilient leaders' first crisis rodeo, the vital post-pandemic church has leaders who are prepared, able, and willing to make the faithful pivots and adaptive changes needed to lead a resilient church. These resilient leaders know how to remain calm and lead from a place of responsiveness (intellect) and not reaction (emotion). Not only do they remain calm, but these leaders and churches help others in the congregation and the community remain calm. When someone leads from a reactionary/emotional place, s/he is not usually making the best decisions or leading from a place of health and wholeness. However, resilient leaders lead from a place of response/intellect and calmness, making much better and healthier choices for themselves, the congregation, and the community they serve.

The Story

A church I was working with encountered three major crises over just a few short months. First, storm water from the local municipality backed up into the church facility, ruining all the carpet and the lower foot of sheet rock on all the walls along with the baseboards. Second, a lightning strike took out most of their technology, alarm system, and some of the electrical connections. Third, a member on break from a church leaders' meeting was assaulted in the church restroom by someone who had wandered in off of the street.

This congregation and its leaders could have easily called it quits. Some would say, "That's three strikes – we're out of here!" Instead, this congregation and specifically its leaders, quickly found an alternative location for worship, moved what furniture and fixtures could be salvaged to a temporary office space, and set out to make all the necessary repairs.

Along with responding to these situations, these resilient leaders also saw opportunity. This was an opportunity for them to embrace the simplified, accountable structure they had newly adopted. They also used this as a time to experiment with their worship experience, worship order, worship leaders, hospitality, connection, etc. Since there was already a disruption in the norm, these resilient leaders took advantage of the situation to experiment. When they did return to their facility, they were able to reopen with a fresh worship experience, including a new integrated hospitality and connection process. Resilient leaders remain calm, find solutions rather than obstacles, and find opportunity in the midst of crisis.

Bottom Line

Resilient churches and resilient leaders are survivors. These resilient organizations and leaders are ones that have pulled themselves up by their own bootstraps on multiple occasions gaining new insights each time. Survivors are often people who see the blessing in survival and therefore have a deep appreciation of the journey, its lessons, and what was made possible because of the journey and survival. They are grateful. Resilient churches and leaders also feel a sense of responsibility to make the best of the post-survival journey and share the lessons learned with others. Vital, effective, relevant, and competent post-pandemic churches are built upon the backs of resilient congregations and its resilient leaders.

Questions to Ponder

1. Thinking about the pandemic crisis, what were some of the first actions taken by your church? Were the actions more reaction or responsive based?

2. Name five or six people in the church who you would label as encouragers. What traits do you identify in her or him that indicates they are an encourager? How has their encouragement affected the congregation as a whole?

3. What other crisis has the church encountered in its history where the church was actually stronger as a result? How was the congregation stronger?

4. Thinking of the typical council or board meeting, is the tendency to find ways for something to work or identify the obstacles? Cite an example.

Resilience Assessment

Consider your current leadership and church culture, how would you rate the overall current level of resilience of your leaders and your congregation? Circle the number below that best represents the overall level of resilience of your leaders AND congregation.

0=No Resilience

10=Very High Resilience

0   1   2   3   4   5   6   7   8   9   10

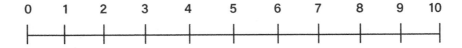

CHAPTER TEN

Courage

According to Dr. Cathy J. Lassiter, 'intellectual courage,' is challenging old assumptions and acting to make changes based on new learnings, understandings and insights gleaned from experience and/or educational research. In the season of Post-COVID, I find the church operating from the posture of intellectual courage. Because COVID-19 has forced the church to change and glean from our spiritual foundation and temporal experiences.

Bishop Sharma D. Lewis
Resident Bishop of the Richmond Episcopal Area of The United Methodist Church

How many times in your church has there been a meeting after the meeting? Often, these "after" meetings are held in the church parking lot and often with people who had nothing to say during the official meeting inside the church. But seemingly, these same people have lots to say at the "after" meeting while standing in the parking lot. I find in the church world that we often lack the courage to make hard decisions, have tough conversations, get out of our comfort zone to try new things, and hold one another accountable to our most important work of making disciples. It appears that we church people need a big ol' dose of courage! Yet, those churches who will be healthy and vital in the post-pandemic world will be very courageous.

Stay alert, stand firm in the faith, show courage, be strong.

1 Corinthians 16:13 (NET)

Tough Conversation Avoidance

In coaching and consulting over the past decade plus with hundreds of churches across the country, it was baffling why church leaders have such difficulty having hard conversations and making difficult decisions. Being a lay person and having worked and led in the business world for two decades, owning my own businesses, I have had to learn to hold those hard conversations. In fact, in the secular world of leaders, if you are not willing and able to have those hard conversations, you will likely not keep your job. Business leaders are expected and trained to have difficult, but necessary conversations. The growth, health, and bottom-line profits will be adversely affected should these conversations be avoided. The cost of avoidance is too high a price to pay for successful business leaders and the companies they represent.

So why is the expectation of leaders being willing and able to have hard conversations and make hard decisions not a common practice in church leadership? After all, leading a church to reach the souls of people who are looking for love, grace, healing, and purpose is the greatest work (ministry) we are called to do. Interestingly, it is sometimes business leaders who are able to have tough conversations in the workplace who are the same leaders that avoid tough conversations in the church.

It took me some time to form this hypothesis of the

issue and be presented the opportunity to test it with some church leadership teams. These experiences have led me to the conclusion that church leaders (clergy and laity alike) avoid hard conversations because we have grown to believe that maintaining relationships with one another inside the church is more important and/or more highly valued than the mission of the church. I am certainly not claiming that this was an intentional decision church leaders made at some specific time. Instead, it has grown to be a part of the culture of many churches. Somehow, it appears many church leaders have come to think that hard conversions are void of grace and love and therefore would not be the "Christian" thing to do. Possibly hurting someone's feelings must therefore be avoided at all cost. Or having the person I sit next to in the same pew every Sunday upset with me for sharing a differing or unpopular thought or opinion on church direction is just not an option.

Avoiding difficult conversations and even avoiding difficult decisions continues to crush so many churches. It is heartbreaking. Avoidance is taking the path of least resistance, instead of being a courageous leader. To think a single conversation or small series of conversations could be the difference between a church thriving and wasting away is heartbreaking. Too many churches unintentionally make decisions for their churches not to thrive by avoiding difficult conversations. Most avoid them for relationally-driven reasons, without consideration for the missionally-driven reasons that might cause them to have the difficult conversations and make the difficult decisions.

Bottom Line

Vital, healthy churches are willing, able, and embrace hard conversations and difficult decisions. They do this because they understand the critical importance and commissioning from Jesus to go and make disciples. They have come to understand that having difficult conversations is part of leadership responsibilities. Hard conversations can also be grace and love-filled conversations. Competent leaders understand that running towards conflict rather than avoiding conflict is a healthy leadership strategy. Conflict is an opportunity for growth, understanding, and clarity. They covenant together as leaders to be accountable to Christ for leading the church to be missionally-focused.

> *Instead, speaking the truth in love, we will grow to become in every respect the mature body of him who is the head, that is, Christ.*
>
> **Ephesians 4:15 (NIV)**

The following are five real life incidences illustrating the avoidance of hard conversations (and making difficult decisions) I have encountered repeatedly, along with the consequences faced by some unhealthy churches not being faithful to the mission:

- Leaders unwilling to address church bullies because the bully has influence, high giving, or has instilled fear of retaliation. The result of not having hard conversations and avoiding difficult decisions has driven off part of the congregation, kept new people from coming or staying, and kept the congregation fearful and paralyzed.

- Leaders unwilling to release a toxic employee. Too often the employee was hired from within the congregation and the employee's congregational ties and influence stop the leaders from having hard conversations and/or making difficult decisions. Leaders choose to keep one toxic employee rather than releasing the toxicity so the church can be healthier and become vital. Protecting one employee has often led to losing many existing people (staff and congregation), stifling ministry, wasting salary dollars, and detouring the church from its mission.

- Leaders unwilling to hold their pastor accountable. Too often laity leaders do not feel worthy or perhaps do not feel they have the authority to hold a pastor accountable. Because of this, those hard conversations and difficult decisions are avoided, leaving an ineffective or unhealthy pastoral leader in place – sometimes for years. Without an agreed-upon vision and goals, church leaders are often unclear on what it means to hold a pastor accountable, or what the pastor is being held accountable for. The consequence of this avoidance is having weakened, unhealthy, overbearing, lazy, and/or ineffective pastoral leadership, which sometimes takes years for a congregation to overcome once the pastor finally leaves. In the meantime, the missional-focus is lost, new people aren't coming to know Jesus, and laity leaders are hard to recruit.

- Leaders unwilling to hold other leaders accountable. This is very similar to the avoidance of pastoral accountability and often has similar consequences at the board or council level or, sometimes, at the ministry team level.

• Not willing to stop a ministry. Programs and ministries are meant to have a life cycle resulting in eventual death. Yet, too often, leaders are unwilling to stop ministries because of the traditional alliance to the ministry – or because of the relational bondage of the ministry – even when it is no longer effective, producing results, and/or missionally focused. The ministry continues because we have always done it. The ministry continues because someone started it and it would be disrespectful to that person if it were stopped. The consequences of the avoidance of this hard conversation or difficult decision result in wasting resources (i.e., time, energy, and dollars) on an activity that has become ineffective and reaching no new disciples. In addition, the ineffective ministry is taking away resources from new or existing ministries that could be missionally-focused and effective.

According to Marlene Chism: "The paradox is that the very act of avoidance also carries an underlying emotional toll. As a leader, no matter what your title, you know when you aren't stepping up to the plate. There's that inner voice that tells you something is off. This is your north star, your compass, your inner alignment. There is cost to the lack of personal alignment: lost sleep, depression, anger, and fear. The real problem is fear of your own and other people's emotions."[9]

---

[9] Chism, Marlene, "The Mega Cost of Avoiding Difficult Conversations," https://marlenechism.com/blog/mega-cost-of-avoiding-difficult-conversations/, February 21, 2017.

It takes courage to be a church leader in today's world. As Christians – and specifically as Christian leaders – we are called to step into our leadership roles and be courageous for the sake of the Gospel. I often close trainings, webinars, and meetings with leaders in prayer, asking God to bless those leaders with boldness and courageousness to lead churches to reach new people as we are called to do. May it be so.

Planter Courage

With the changing landscape, the traditional models of effective church planting are shifting. The "parachute drop strategy" of church planting is nearly non-existent. It's just too expensive, risky, and taking too long to become self-sustaining. There is a growing movement involving house churches, micro-churches, and missional communities. These newer planter strategies provide an opportunity for greater laity involvement, less overhead, more organic growth, less clergy-dependence, and generally more attractive to Generations Y and Z. These smaller gatherings are also a more widely accepted means of gathering due to the fear of larger gatherings brought on by the pandemic.

Just because these are smaller gatherings doesn't mean the opportunity for tremendous growth is not possible. Networks of these smaller gatherings are developing, bringing with them the resources, training, and infrastructure to support these movements. This is all great news! But what this means is that denominational judicatory leaders will need to greatly shift how they have traditionally gone about identifying, equipping, and deploying church planters, along with the associated funding strategies and expectations. This means more traditional models will need to yield to the movements of smaller gatherings – along with the possibility of strictly online ministry, social entrepreneurs, faith communities, marketplace ministries, etc.

To be a church planter in the post-pandemic world will take great courage. There is no one tried and true strategy for "church planting" and this is especially true in this new post-pandemic world. While church planting has never been a low-risk venture, there will be more risk in the post-pandemic church as church planters and denominational leaders alike adapt and innovate to reach new people in new ways. Yet, less of the world's population is part of a faith community, so the opportunities are exponential in how many people can be reached. Now is our opportunity to be bold and courageous in exploring strategies for reaching new people in new ways through church planting.

Bishop Lewis[10] offers her favorite scripture on courage:

> *"Be strong and courageous. Do not be afraid or terrified because of them, for the Lord your God goes with you; he will never leave your nor forsake you"*
>
> **Deuteronomy 31:6 (NIV)**

---

[10] Bishop Sharma D. Lewis, Resident Bishop of the Richmond Episcopal Area of The United Methodist Church

Vulnerability as an Explorer

Just as with church planting, established faith communities will need to be courageous as they adapt and innovate in the post-pandemic world to be on mission. It is essential to risk vulnerability as we navigate the new cultures and times. This vulnerability needs to include openness to failing on the way to succeeding, opening up to new relationships in the community, exploring new ministries and programs and last – but not least – the willingness to stop ministries that are no longer missionally effective, leaving resources to invest in new ministries that are effective.

"Exposed," "unarmed," "unguarded," and "unprotected" are common words used to describe vulnerability. These are not terms normally used to describe the church. Yet, this openness to be exposed – as sinful people who are trying to do their best to follow Jesus and grow in discipleship – is what is attractive to those we are trying to reach. The rawness and honesty that comes with vulnerability as individuals and as Christians is the real-ness and authenticity people who have been traditionally resistant to the church crave.

People's "BS" meter is highly sensitive, and folks will run when there is just a hint of inauthenticity or lack of transparency. We Christians are not always great at sharing our flaws, being transparent, and being real with people – especially new people. Yet, those faith communities that will be missionally effective in the post-pandemic world will be filled with people who are willing to be vulnerable, because their hearts are breaking for those who have not yet heard the Good News.

Passion

Passion brings about energy, excitement, and curiosity. When someone brings passion to a conversation or subject, people lean in a bit closer and listen a bit more intently. Nelson Mandela said:

There is no passion to be found playing small – in settling for a life that is less than the one you are capable of living.

Leaders who exude passion are leaders who are more likely to be followed. Who wants to follow a leader who is lukewarm and humdrum with no energy and excitement? Not me.

Passionate people build churches full of passionate followers of Jesus. Passion is often driven by a God-given vision. In turn, that vision will drive excitement, momentum, generosity, and vitality. Passion is about intensity, enthusiasm, and excitement. Passion is often the driver that springs people out of bed each day. Vital churches in the post-pandemic world create a culture that ignites passion in the congregation, leading to a passionate movement of people who can't help but exude that passion with the people they encounter in their daily lives. In turn, those they encounter will want to be a part of the same vision.

The Story

I once had the great pleasure of working with a man who was the epitome of a courageous leader. He was nearing what is typically considered the twilight years of his ministry – where many leaders could coast into retirement. He was leading a stable congregation that was healthy, but not necessarily growing. Still, this leader had an undeniable drive.

He was sure God was calling him to finish strong. Finishing strong didn't mean simply keeping his foot off the break. No! To him, finishing strong meant putting the pedal to the metal! He did just that in a monumental way.

This courageous leader boldly walked his congregational leaders through a discernment process that began by opening themselves up to becoming a multi-site faith community. Secondly, this courageous leader – along with the support of his congregational leaders – decided to partner with an unhealthy congregation that was highly conflicted. Patiently walking alongside this dying congregation with lively resistance was a selfless act of vulnerability, wrapped in a passion for reaching new people. With a deep helping of persistence, prayer, and grace-filled conversations, this brave and courageous leader led this highly conflicted congregation through a process towards agreeing to become a second site of the larger, stable congregation.

Not every leader would have taken on such a hard task, let alone do so later in ministry. Yet, it was because this leader was willing to be vulnerable – driven by his passion for reaching new people – that this second site now has the chance to become a vital faith community, able to reach people they had been unable to reach for decades.

Bottom Line

Being a vital church in the post-pandemic world is not for wimpy leaders looking for a safe place to land and be comfortable. A vital church will not survive leaders who want to sit in their offices or studies, hiding from relationships. There's no time for heads buried in books, playing ministry safe. Courageous leaders are needed who are willing to take risks, be vulnerable, instill passion, have hard conversations, and make difficult decisions. Leaders, who in turn, will be more effective in leading vital, growing, healthy churches.

Questions to Ponder

1. In thinking about the history of your faith community, how has avoiding hard conversations played into the vitality of the church and its effectiveness in being missionally focused?

2. In thinking about the history of your faith community, how has avoiding difficult decisions played into the vitality of your church and its effectiveness in being missionally focused?

3. Describe a recent example of how the church has been vulnerable. How was this perceived and received by the congregation?

4. Recall a ministry in the life of the church where a passion sparked a movement that moved the mission forward.

Vulnerability Assessment

Consider your current leadership and church culture, how would you rate the overall current level of vulnerability of your leaders and your congregation? Circle the number below that best represents the level of vulnerability level of both the leaders AND the congregation.

0=No Vulnerability

10=High Vulnerability

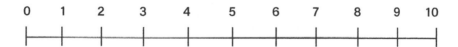

Next Steps

CHURCH

a human connection of love,
not a building

a lifestyle,
not a weekly activity

an act of service,
not a service to attend

Taylor DuVall

The post-pandemic church must be different than what it was prior to 2020. To lead the church forward, leaders can't be frozen in a pre-pandemic world. The future church and its leaders will need to be flexible, relational, visionary, spiritually grounded, highly committed, innovative, resilient, and courageous. These were likely not the practices most churches regularly practiced or valued prior to the pandemic. The attributes of leaders with these practices and traits were not necessarily the traits the church searched for, valued, or even encouraged.

But friends, please hear me. For us Christ followers, trying to do our part in living out the Great Commission and the Great Commandment, we must release what we have previously been and done. It no longer works. We must do better. We must be better. We must begin to re-imagine what it means to be the church.

The pandemic was a horrific, historical, and devastating long-term occurrence. It will take years, possibly decades, to discover the totality of the ripple effects of this pandemic. Yet conversely, this sudden disruption of life as we once knew it has given the church a wonderful, unprecedented opportunity to rethink, re-imagine, and reinvent the church.

Unfortunately, not every church or every church leader will see the opportunity, let alone reap the opportunities that will arise as a result. It is likely those who are flexible, relational, visionary, spiritually grounded, highly committed, innovative, resilient, and courageous will be the ones that recognize and respond to the opportunity for a church reformation.

Being the church of 1820 did not determine what the church would be in 1920, 1960, 1980, 2000, or let alone 2020. Each generation and decade revealed a need for the church to relate with culture in different ways as the culture has shifted. This never meant sacrificing or watering down the Good News. It simply meant being of the people – doing life with the people you are trying to reach in – real ways.

The people of a faith community can't be separated or compartmentalized from the people in the mission field they are called to reach for Jesus Christ. In contrast, vital churches in the post-pandemic world are woven into the fabric of their mission fields and have a heartbreaking urgency with missional focus and priority. The only thing sacred is The Word. Everything else is to be leveraged, revamped, re-purposed, and invested in making sure more people are introduced to The Word and discipled as followers of Jesus Christ.

Churches that will survive and thrive are churches who practice the traits outlined in this book. While not all nine traits are required, it typically takes more than a trait or two to be truly missionally effective and vital. One trait builds on another and, collectively, these nine traits are the powerhouse for being a vital church, fulfilling the Great Commission in new ways, reaching new people, in this new post-pandemic world.

A Call for Action

I am ever so grateful and humbled that you have invested in this resource with your dollars, time, focus, and energy. But, this is only the beginning. Having read some words – maybe even being challenged by them – will not answer the call God has placed on us as disciples who have been put in this post-pandemic world for such a time as this. To answer the call to becoming a more vital congregation in this post-pandemic world requires action with a sense of passion and urgency. To create your church's unique action plan, let's start first with writing down the assessment numbers from each chapter below. I truly pray the assessments were completed only after a holy conversation around the chapter questions was first conducted. If those conversations with other congregational leaders have not yet occurred, I urge you to circle back to those questions and conversations which lead you to a more holistic assessment approach.

> *The same holds true for you: since you are ambitious for spiritual gifts, use your ambition to try to work toward being the best at building up the church.*
>
> **1 Corinthians 14:12 (CEB)**

Creating an Action Plan

Copy the assessment numbers (ranging from 0-10) from Chapters Three through Ten below.

_____ Flexible

_____ Relational

_____ Visionary

_____ Spiritually grounded

_____ Highly committed

_____ Innovative

_____ Resilient

_____ Courageous

Identify the top traits with the highest assessment scores. Write these three traits in the spaces below listing the trait with the highest assessment score first.

_____

_____

_____

Next, identify the traits with the lowest assessment scores. Write these three traits in the spaces below starting the list with the trait with the lowest assessment score first.

_____

_____

_____

Next, identify the remaining traits that did not fall into the top or bottom scores. Write these three traits in the spaces below starting the list with the trait with the highest assessment score first.

_____

_____

_____

Where do we start? While it is often our instinct to begin our work on those traits that present our largest gaps, I would challenge us to build on our strengths. Take a look again at the top-rated traits. How can you take those top-rated traits up a couple of notches? What conversations need to take place? What brave decisions need to be made? What do we need to let go of and what do we need to grab? What type of pastoral and laity leaders will need to be in place for these shifts to occur?

Next take a look at those traits that fell into the middle of our assessments. Again, what would we need to do to nudge those numbers up so we could live into those traits that will allow us to be a more vital congregation? How can we be more missionally focused?

> *If you don't know where you are going,*
> *you'll end up someplace else.*
>
> **Yogi Berra**
> former New York Yankees catcher

Let me offer a word of encouragement and caution. Increasing the scores on these traits will result in changing the culture of your congregation. This does not happen overnight. It will take patience and persistence and will likely be met with some resistance. Still, we need to balance these with a sense of urgency. Without a sense of urgency, we will likely not make the necessary cultural shifts inside the congregation quickly enough to survive in the post-pandemic world. It is a difficult balance, but so worth it for the sake of the mission. If you are finding it difficult to navigate these action steps, consider hiring a church coach for your board or council who is experienced in effectively leading churches and its leaders through congregational transformation. This can prove to be an invaluable investment to have a neutral experienced coach with fresh eyes and ears walk alongside your leaders as you work your Action Plan for building up and practicing these vital traits for a healthy post-pandemic church.

What will you begin to embrace as a church and as a faith leader to thrive for the sake of Jesus? Where will you begin? What is your congregation's first step? When will this be finished? What is the second faithful step? When will it be finished? In my experience, without a plan there will be no intentional outcome. A plan starts with a first step. Plan your first step now in becoming a vital, healthy, missionally focused church in the post-pandemic world!

Our Church's Action Plan

Step One   Completion Date

Step Two   Completion Date

Step Three   Completion Date

Note the Current Church Assessment number you recorded in
Chapter Two on page 21. As you work your Action Plan, come back
to these assessment questions and the resulting rating number
from time to time. This will help you see the progress you are
making towards becoming a more vital and effective church in the
post-pandemic world.

The RE Playbook
RElaunching Your Church in the Post-Pandemic World

Kay L. Kotan

INTRODUCTION

RE ...

Whether your church is preparing to REengage in in-person worship or you have been gathering in-person again for weeks or months, it is time for RE. RE is a Playbook for the church as we enter into a post-pandemic world. There are few things (if any) that are the same now as they were pre-pandemic. We have just encountered a historical event like no other. Everything has changed, including the church. We can try to convince ourselves that the church remains unaffected, but we would be in complete denial. The world has changed. The culture has changed. Therefore, we as individuals can't escape being affected. Since individuals make up the church, the church, too, has changed. Like it or not, that's where we are. It is time to face the reality and respond with faithful obedience as the church.

As your church emerges into the post-pandemic world, we find ourselves in a unique situation. What was is no more. But what will be has not yet arrived. The church is in a rare season of possibility. Our challenge is to take advantage of this season by doing the faithful work of discernment, forward thinking, and strategizing. While our tendency might very well be to retreat back to the practices and traditions of comfort and familiarity, we must instead resist the tendency and instead seize the opportunity.

You are being invited into a journey. The journey is one of discovery. A discovery of how God is uniquely calling your church into this post-pandemic world. We ask you to be in a place of openness, curiosity, boldness, and willingness to consider being the church in a new way in this new emerging day. We ask you to engage in the hard conversations that will come from your learnings that could result in new church pivots, shifts, revitalization, and missional focus.

We are REminded:

- The church can't ignore this holy disruption or we risk becoming **_more_** culturally irrelevant.
- The pandemic catapulted technology integration and adoption into the future by a decade or more. The church can't afford to ignore or refuse to embrace it.
- Crisis doesn't *create* failure; it accelerates it. Crisis doesn't *create* momentum; it accelerates the momentum that was already there.

The RE journey can help your church use this season as one of REcreating itself. REentry into the community. A time to consider REcalibration needs. A chance to RElate to your community in a new, more meaningful way. An opportunity to REcommit the church to its mission and purpose with new focus and intention. A season to RElaunch the church into the neighborhood REclaiming who we are and whose we are.

The RE Playbook focuses on four major REset areas including:

REcalibrating

RElating

REcommitting

RElaunching.

As the RE Team, church leaders invest in the future church as they utilize the RE Playbook. The beginning of each section will offer insights and shifts for the RE Team's consideration. At the end of each section, the RE Team will find a RE Team Responds area to REflect on current REality, REveal a new direction, and REshape the church to answer the call that God is calling the congregation into REnewal, using the four REsets.

Gather your RE Team and let's start our journey to Post-Pandemic REformation.

REset One

REcalibrate with the Seasons

As we consider our REentry as the church, we are challenged to consider the possibilities that might lie before us. Imagine gazing through a lens as if we were a new church plant. What opportunities could be before us if we REorient ourselves, thinking of the congregation as a new church plant rather than "going back" to the established church and the "way things were?" This REfreshing perspective enables us to REconsider options that might not otherwise be on the table.

Church planters recognize seven seasons of "planting." These include:

- Discerning

- Visioning

- Gathering

- Discipling

- Worshiping

- Maturing

- Multiplying

If we were to apply these same seasons to the established church as we RElaunch for these new times, these REfined definitions RElate to the seven seasons.

Discerning

A congregational call to deep, intentional prayer. In her book, Open Road[1], Sue Nilson Kibbey refers to this as a breakthrough prayer initiative. It is a time of asking God to break through and open doors to new hopes, dreams, and possibilities for our church.

Visioning

This is a clear, distinct picture of the future God is calling on the church to become. It is the unique method in which your church lives out its purpose: its mission of making disciples as called for in the Great Commission. Vision provides momentum, energy, and a common charge behind which the congregation can rally.

Gathering

This season is a time of building new relationships with new people from the community who have a shared energy and excitement for the vision. One person begins building relationships and – through invitation to be on the journey together – those who were invited begin inviting others. Soon there is a whole team of networkers, inviting new people into conversation, building relationships, and entering ministry together to fulfill the vision.

---

1   Sue Nilson Kibbey, *Open Road,* Market Square Books, 2021.

Discipling

Those gathered disciple one another in their maturing faith in following Jesus Christ. They hold one another accountable for their on-going discipleship journey and urge each in their continued growth in becoming disciple-making disciples.

Worshiping

We are created to be in relationship with one another and with God. As humans we have worship embedded in our human nature. We express the loving of our Lord-God with all of our heart through worship. Worship is designed with the mission field in mind, taking into consideration their interests, desires, and needs.

Maturing

This is a season of growing people and healthy systems to support and enable the mission and vision. This includes growing people in discipleship and leadership with a multiplication expectation.

Multiplying

Healthy organisms grow and multiply. Healthy churches grow and multiply, too. Vital congregations multiply disciples, leaders, ministries, and faith communities. Multiplication is part of the church DNA and therefore comes naturally.

RElaunch Playbook: Knowing which season of development the church is in will provide insights into what areas of focus and development need attention.

As a coach to both new church plants/planters and established churches/pastors, I wish all clergy were equipped to be church planters. How wonderful would it be for us to have a DNA of multiplication with church plants and with established congregations? Can you imagine the profound impact this would have beyond churches, but on the world as a whole? If we had not lost this culture of multiplication of sharing the Good News, our world would be profoundly transformed and different. We would be a much more faith-based culture, doing our best to exhibit and practice the fruits of the spirit. What a world that would be!

Take some time to RE-read the seven seasons as you prepare to REspond with your RE Team.

RE Team REsponds

REflect

1. As you REflect on the seven seasons, what seasons are fully formed in your congregation?

2. Which seasons are still immature and need REvisited?

3. If you were a new church start, would you be REady for the worshiping season? What brings you to this conclusion?

REveal

1. What has been REvealing to you as you REflect on the seasons and your congregation's maturity in each?

2. What strengths and gaps of your congregation have been REvealed in learning about the seven seasons?

3. What possibilities excite you most as you think about how the seasons could speak into the future of your congregation and a RElaunch? What concerns you?

REshape to RElaunch

1. Based on your REading, REflecting through questions, and REvealing conversations, what needs to be REshaped as you consider next faithful steps?

2. What is your first step you have identified that needs to be REshaped?

3. Who is responsible for the REshaping? What is the timeframe for the REshaping?

REset Two

RElate

The church is in the RElationship "business." We are in RElationship with one another as brothers and sisters in Christ. We are in RElationship with Jesus Christ. The level of engagement by any person in the life and ministry of a congregation is largely determined by the level of RElational connections they experience. Through these RElationships, more people are introduced to Christ and become disciples. Disciples become disciple makers. The cycle continues. That is, the cycle continues as long as we continue to build new RElationships and don't become insular. Too often, churches begin to focus on those already gathered, ignore those newly gathered, and forget about those who are yet to be gathered.

As we consider options to REset RElationships, we need to be REminded that the whole purpose for the church is to become a sending station of people to go and train others in the way of Christ. If we limit ourselves to caring for those already gathered, how can we be the full expression of the church? When our primary focus is first on those yet to be gathered, the already gathered and newly gathered take care of themselves, for the most part. When we make a priority for those already gathered, however, the other two groups cease to exist. The church is stagnant at best, and likely in decline.

RElaunch Playbook: Relationships are at the core of what the church is to be about. RElationships with those yet to be gathered must be our primary focus.

Hospitality

Most new RElationships start with some expression of hospitality. Think about your fondest memories formed with friends. Likely it is grounded in some initial offering of hospitality: a phone call, a note, an invitation, dinner, a shared experience or adventure, etc. In American culture, we have all come to expect some sort of general hospitality. For example, when entering a restaurant, we expect to be greeted, seated, offered menus, served with promptness and efficiency, good food, drinks refilled without delay or asking, the check offered on a timely basis, cleanliness, comfortable seating, etc. Those are all things we have come to *expect* yet we refer to this not as *expectations* but as the offering of hospitality. Radical or extravagant hospitality is exceeding expectations - going above and beyond.

Churches often believe they are offering the best of hospitality. Yet, we are likely only meeting people's expectations. It is not an offering of extravagant or radical hospitality. It is not necessarily memorable or leads a new person to take notice or feel as though they were a "guest of honor." Think back to some of your restaurant experiences. What are some of the extravagant or radical "over the top" experiences you have had? How would those types of experiences play out in the life of the church? How could we offer extravagant hospitality to first-time guests?

Whether a person experiences the church through online worship, in-person worship, a small group, or part of an organization who uses the church facility, the church should be offering extravagant hospitality. We often think about hospitality only for the in-person Sunday morning worship service. What about people using the facility (i.e., scouts, exercise classes, daycare, preschool, voters, community groups, funeral attendees, food pantry) throughout the week? What about those attending online worship or other ministry opportunities? As people in the RElationship business, we will want to ensure we are modeling extravagant hospitality!

For example, consider the pre-Covid in-person Sunday morning hospitality experience. What intentional offerings of extravagant hospitality were in place? Write them down.

- Next, consider how to translate the hospitality offered in-person (or desired to be offered) to online worship.

- What replaces the parking lot greeter?

- What replaces the door greeters?

- What replaces the pre-service gathering in the lobby?

- What replaces the pre-service gathering time in the sanctuary?

- What replaces the meet and greet time?

- What replaces the connection card?

- What replaces the connection center?

- What replaces coffee and donuts?

Now consider how extravagant hospitality – as the first step in building a RElationship – might be offered to anyone who encounters the church *at any time.*

Next, consider how extravagant hospitality is being offered on the church website and through social media. Develop an intentional approach of extravagant, 24/7,hospitality for all church-related activities.

RElaunch Playbook: Hospitality is expected in the secular world. Extravagant hospitality is what the church – as a whole and individually as disciples of Christ – should be modeling as an act of "loving thy neighbor as yourself" and as a first step in building new RElationships.

Already Gathered

As we REview relationships, let's begin with those already gathered. This is your church's congregation. During the height of the pandemic, Barna reported that approximately one-third of those who had been regular attenders pre-pandemic were no longer attending church at all - online or in-person. This likely means there will be a need to REconnect with your already-gathered people post-pandemic. Consider the intentional methods you could be using to REconnect such as phone calls, written notes, emails, care packages, special ministry offerings, etc. People will need to know they are/were missed. There needs to be opportunities for them to REengage and RElate again.

How is your church prayer team praying for the congregation individually and collectively? How are we teaching the congregation to pray for one another in their personal daily prayer time as well as calling one another on the phone to pray for each other? How are we praying for guidance on how to stay connected or REeconnect with those who were already gathered?

Caring and supporting our brothers and sisters in Christ is an essential part of being in Christian community with one another. Yet, we minimize the amount of care a church can provide if the only care provider is the pastor. Indeed, the pastor should be showing up for the moments of emergency, crisis, and momentous occasions. But we need to shift from pastoral care to congregational care if we are to become or remain a vital church.

Providing simple and easy ways for our existing – as well as newly gathered people – to give generously is important. Collecting tithes and offerings only by passing the offering plate is a limiting practice for churches. It limits the options for giving. Depending on which study you read, more than half, and sometimes up to two-thirds, of people polled do not carry cash. Even less carry a checkbook with them. The numbers grow larger when looking specifically at those in their 20-30's. When the pandemic hit, those churches who only collected offerings through the passed plate had to scramble to find alternative giving methods when worship went online. Those churches who already had alternative giving options such as monthly automated withdrawals, QR codes, credit cards, etc. were ahead of the curve and had far fewer people to REdirect or RE-educate on how to give.

It is the REsponsibility of the church to provide discipling opportunities for our already gathered people. This starts with having an intentional faith development pathway (discipleship pathway). Next, we build a culture of expectation of attenders and members. This leads these persons on a continuous journey of deepening their faith as they become more deeply committed followers of Christ, sharingtheirfaith with others. Whether we are gathering in-person, online, or both, providing steps and expectations in discipleship is absolutely essential.

RElaunch Playbook: For those already gathered, we need to pay attention to REconnection, prayer, congregational care, giving options, and intentional and expected discipleship.

Newly Gathered

When the pandemic hit, those who were already gathered in local churches for in-person worship likely had to make a fast and hard pivot to online worship. Without any intentionality (or perhaps even REalization), the church launched a second site. The church became multi-site overnight. Granted, many churches did this out of desperation to provide "something" for those already gathered, rather than following a strategic plan. Nonetheless, a second site was launched. And again, without intention, some churches actually attracted new people to view the online worship experience. Great!

For those newly gathered people, how did we intentionally RElate? How did we offer extravagant hospitality? How did we intentionally try to connect RElationally and authentically? If we REcorded a worship experience and uploaded it for viewing, but had no intentional opportunities to connect, we missed a tremendous opportunity. We forgot we were in the RElationship business. We forgot we moved out of the building and launched a second site.

Unfortunately, if this were an in-person worship service, the experience would be like a first-time guest showing up, no one speaking to her/him, no one making eye contact, and no one engaging to show any desire to connect in any way. We would never consider treating an in-person worship guest in this manner, some churches did just this by the method in which they were offering online worship. It was as if we were delivering a "service," rather than offering a desired and intentional opportunity to RElate to God and others.

Another way to think about this is to consider that the church has entered into a ripe mission field full of unchurched people. The mission field is the digital world, with an estimated 70 percent population of unchurched people of all ages and stages of life. Yet, with this ripe harvest before us, we missed (or are missing) the opportunity to harvest because we did it for those already gathered as the focus, rather than the yet to be gathered.

Another question for consideration relates to whether we are/were offering online worship or online ministry. Online worship is the 30–60 minute worship experience usually offered/posted once a week. Online ministry is the full expression of the life of the church offered digitally. In other words, online ministry encompasses extravagant hospitality, optional methods for giving, connection, engagement options, discipleship, service opportunities, prayer, and faith-sharing. Did/does your church offer online worship or online ministry?

While there was already a growing concern around the number of people who reported being lonely, depressed, or anxious, the pandemic escalated those numbers significantly. People are hungry for community. People are aching to connect with others in meaningful ways. At one time, people found this type of community and connection in their local church. But because the church has become culturally irrelevant to so many, the church is no longer the "third place" (work and home being the first and second) where people do life. During the pandemic, not only was the church not the third place, but often work was eliminated as a second place. Most people were left to do life in only one place: home. Isolated - at home. For months. No wonder people are lonelier and more depressed!

We used to gauge church vitality based on the average number of people who attended in-person worship. While that might have been helpful to some degree, using attendance as a vitality barometer grew increasingly less effective as congregants' attendance patterns decreased. While regular attendance used to equate to weekly attendance, regular attendance pre-pandemic decreased to about once a month. It became apparent during the pandemic, that many of those who were regular attenders pre-pandemic were no longer attending church at all (online or in-person).

We have now come to understand that worship attendance does not necessarily equate to discipleship growth. While participation in a small discipleship group led to increasing frequency of worship attendance, the opposite – that increasing frequency in worship attendance leads to discipleship growth – was not always true. Therefore, we need to re-examine how to measure ministry effectiveness and fruitfulness.

The emerging trend is that evaluating and measuring engagement is the better barometer. Engagement speaks to an individual's discipleship development. How are the newly gathered connected to other people in the gathered community? Perhaps by engaging with other newly gathered? How do we help them engage in ministry (serve)? How do we help them find and engage the discipleship pathway? How do we help them take their next faithful step on that pathway? How do we help them continue to take additional steps? How are we offering mentors/coaches to pick them up when they trip on their faith journey? How are we offering models of mature disciples?

RElaunch Playbook: For those newly gathered, we need to intentionally and authentically provide RElational connections to help them engage in ministry and discipleship in meaningful ways.

Yet to Be Gathered

Because we are in the disciple-making business – which is accomplished through RElationships – our primary focus, attention, energy, and resources should be on those yet to be gathered. Those yet to be gathered are unchurched people God is calling us to reach.

In a pandemic world, some were quick to REject the possibility of REaching new people while the world was in quarantine. Yet, there are many options to connect with new people, even in pandemic times. Here are just a few examples:

- **Watch parties** - Build a culture for those attending online worship to host watch parties inviting their online friends to join them for worship.

- **Invite others** - Believe it or not, a surprising number of people said they would attend church with someone they knew if they were invited. Invite a friend to join you!

- **Already gathered, starting new groups** – Those who were already gathered have a great opportunity to connect with unchurched neighbors in new ways. Whether this was a neighborhood curb party (neighbors stayed in their respective driveways and talked to nearby neighbors), parents gathering virtually to support other parents trying to juggle working from home while homeschooling children, cooks gathering with other cooks sharing recipes as more people were cooking at home, launching a neighborhood care group for picking up groceries or prescriptions for those unable to get out, online happy hour, online book clubs, etc.

- Post a picture contest

- Trivia challenges

- Devotionals/reflections

- Virtual mystery parties

- Bible study podcasts

- Virtual music concerts

- Neighborhood driveway dance-offs

The possibilities are endless! Find a need or shared purpose/desire and invite people to join! It is that simple.

Also be sure to review the previous hospitality and newly gathered section to ensure your church is RElating, connecting, and offering next steps for the newly gathered, too. Consider this for both the online community as well as the in-person community.

> **RElaunch Playbook:** The yet to be gathered are to be the primary focus of the church. Mature disciples are modeling this through their own focus, attention, inviting, and discipling new people continuously.

RE Team REsponds

REflect

1. REflecting on your pre-pandemic hospitality, how would you rate your church's level of hospitality? During your current online worship and your current in-person worship (if applicable)?

2. How is our church doing in RElating (in its fullest expression) to those already gathered, newly gathered, and yet to be gathered? What is one faithful step to RElating more deeply for those already gathered, those newly gathered, and those yet to be gathered?

3. What is the current priority order of already gathered, newly gathered, and yet to be gathered? What brings you to this conclusion?

REveal

1. What is the largest gap in RElating you have identified?

2. How would you describe the RElational culture of your church for those already gathered? For those newly gathered? For those yet to be gathered?

3. What is your church's discipleship pathway? How do people become engaged in the pathway?

REshape to RElaunch

1. What improvements does your church want/need to make in offering extravagant hospitality before RElaunch?

2. Identify the next faithful step to RElate to those already gathered, those newly gathered, and those yet to be gathered.

3. How will your church measure and monitor engagement levels of all three of the "gathered" communities? How will your church prioritize the yet to be gathered community to be faithful to the Great Commission?

REset Three

REcommit

The emphasis of those yet to be gathered is covered in the RElate section of the RE Playbook. You might be wondering why we are now dedicating a whole new section on this RElated topic.

Here's why: In my experience, the majority of churches will likely need to take advantage of the window of opportunity the pandemic offers to make some major shifts. These shifts include a REcommitment to the mission field (the community your church is called and therefore takes responsibility to reach). Here is how I describe this REcommitment:

> *A fresh understanding, devotion, and obligation to the mission field to build authentic relationships, meet needs, and introduce people to Jesus.*

We must first start with naming and claiming the mission field. In other words, what area of town/city is God calling you to reach, and your church is willing to take the responsibility for reaching? Is it a zip code? A school district? City limits? A county? A certain road, bridge, railroad track, river, or highway to the north, south, east, and west? Spend some time with other leaders to discuss and discern. Name it.

A note of caution: Often churches choose a huge mission field with a large population. Resist this urge. The more densely populated the area surrounding (i.e., urban) your facility, the smaller the mission field size should be. In sparsely populated areas (i.e., rural), the mission field is typically a larger area. For example, if the mission field you have identified has a population of 40,000-50,000, your selected area is too large. Typically, you shouldn't designate an area with a population more than about 10,000. Always err on the side of a smaller population, rather than a larger.

Why is the size of the mission field important? The further out we move away from the church and capture greater population, the more diluted the neighborhood information becomes. We are likely to misunderstand our local neighborhood demographics if the population further away has a different primary demographic. If we aren't able to REach the neighbor across the street, it will be much more difficult to REach people at the furthest point of the mission field. Furthermore, the church was built and remains in the neighborhood to first connect with that particular neighborhood. If your church is unwilling or unable to REach the neighborhood in which the church sits, then your congregation needs to consider moving aside and inviting a congregation or a new church planter to take over your location who will connect and build RElationships with its neighbors.

RElaunch Playbook: Naming, claiming, and taking responsibility for introducing the neighborhood to Jesus Christ is key. It places faces on neighbors and helps us understand who they are and how we can best come alongside them as both a neighbor and a faith community.

Once the mission field has been identified, we need to become community experts in knowing our neighbors. What is the primary demographic within your mission field? What are their needs? What keeps them up at night? How could the church be helpful? Who is your neighbor? How will you REcommit to the neighborhood (mission field)? How can we best RElate by knowing their needs? How will we let them know we care? How will we build RElationships? How will we offer opportunities to build RElationships?

Spend time with community leaders learning about the neighborhood and how the church can help and be more RElatable. Claim it.

Next, we must become a part of the community. Live in the mission field. Do business in the mission field. Shop in the mission field. Make new friends in the mission field. Gone are the days of living outside the mission field Monday through Saturday, thinking we can still relate and understand the life of our neighbors in the mission field. This is the work of the congregation - not just the pastor. Pastor, you need to model. Laity, your pastor can't and shouldn't do this alone. Take responsibility.

Don't forget to use local demographic information from the local Chamber of Commerce or other organization to help with this process. Additionally, use resources such as Mission Insite's Full Report, Ministry Insites, Religious Insites, and Mission Impact Guide to first identify and then take a deep dive into learning about your targeted mosaic (a specific demographic group). What type of leadership, worship, hospitality, facility, technology, small groups, learning, and service your targeted demographic aligns with is right at your fingertips! In fact, information on their preferences in communication, books, magazines, websites, television programs, leisure time activities, special interests and more is at your disposal. Become the community expert.

Now that we have gained information through study and conversations with community leaders, it is now time to test the validity of the information. Begin to have conversations with the targeted demographic in the neighborhood (the identified mission field). Be curious. Ask questions. Be open, attentive, and listen deeply. Ask lots of questions. This is the chance to build new RElationships and truly understand who they are, what they desire, and how to connect with them and their peers. This is also a time to hear what community initiative this targeted demographic is passionate about and would like to be involved with in partnership with the church.

After we have invested time in becoming community experts and making new friends within our mission field, we must now invest in some strategic planning. Nothing new happens without being intentional. There are tremendous opportunities before us. Create a strategic plan to REcommit to the mission field. Go back to the RElate sections for reminders, if needed. Hire a coach familiar with REvitalization, RE-launch, and/or new church plants to help you if needed. Invest in this opportunity now so that you don't let this opportunity pass you by.

Here are some considerations for the strategic ministry plan:

- How will we know if we are being effective?

- How will we measure progress?

- What ministries need to be established?

- What might we have to stop in order to have the capacity to offer the new ministries to our neighbors?

- What forms of community need to be offered to help meet the needs of our neighbors?

- How might the church facility need to be REpurposed to meet community needs?

- How will the congregation be dispatched into the neighborhood to serve?

- How will the assets of the congregation be aligned and leveraged to RElate, connect, and engage the neighbors in the mission field? These assets include time, energy, dollars, staff, equipment, endowments, etc. For example, churches who are vital and growing are finding that a complete staffing realignment is required. This includes shifts in such positions of technology and communications becoming priority over other paid staff positions.

RElaunch Playbook: Without a strategic ministry plan, we will not likely create nor implement the desired or intended RElaunch. Instead, we will be REminded of how we have REtracted once again into our building and ignored the community. There will be no pilot, crew, jet fuel, or flight plan for our RElaunch. Instead, we will have likely encountered a fizzled-out dud of a bottle rocket that never took flight.

Now is the time to begin thinking about how to be RElational AND how we will RElaunch into the community later with our new friends.

RE Team REsponds

REflect

1. How many people living in the immediate neighborhood surrounding the church are currently involved in the life of the church? How has that shifted from 10, 20, or 30 years ago?

2. REflecting on the current church budget, what percentage of the budget is specifically dedicated to reaching new people in the neighborhood (those yet to be gathered)?

3. Take a look at the definition offered for REcommitment at the beginning of this section. How committed is the leadership to this REcommitment?

REveal

1. When was the last time your congregation took a deep dive into researching, digesting, and understanding the demographics of your mission field? What are your thoughts about the timing? What does the timing REveal to you?

2. What does the percentage of the budget allocated to the Great Commission REveal to you?

3. What information and understanding has been missing from the church's REality of the mission field and how the assets align with REaching the mission field?

REshape to RElaunch

1. What steps need to be taken to have a comprehensive understanding of the targeted mosaic within the identified mission field?

2. When will the strategic ministry planning be scheduled to complete for RElaunch? Who will do so? What needs careful consideration during the strategic ministry planning? How will leadership ensure the assets are aligned with the strategic ministry plan?

3. What kind of communication, information, and education offerings are needed to bring the congregation along with the strategic ministry plan?

REset Four

RElaunch

Now that we have RE-calibrated our interpretation of the church, REfreshed our understanding of how to RElate, and have declared a REcommitment to the neighborhood, it is time to think about our RElaunch. RElaunch is not just about REsuming in-person worship. RElaunch is much more. Let's REthink all that is possible in a RElaunch.

Consider the following aspects when you create your plan and timing for RElaunch:

- Priority one is to assemble a Prayer Team to pray for the RElaunch, the RElaunch team, the neighborhood, and the yet to be gathered.

- How will you honor those that will no longer be with you as a congregation when you come together in-person (i.e., pandemic-related deaths or deaths by natural cause but congregants unable to attend funerals)? How will you provide care for those mourning?

- How will you prepare the congregation, clergy, staff, and leaders for the likely potential of not seeing some congregants return due to fear of gathering in groups, a decision to worship online, or having found another faith community?

- How will your congregation intentionally RElaunch the church into the community? Will this be a community activity beyond worship (i.e., block party, drive-in movie night, post-pandemic coming outside event, outdoor concert, parade, etc.)? Keep in mind this is to be appealing to the not yet gathered more so than those already gathered.

- How are you inviting and RElating to those who are newly gathered during the RElaunch planning and implementation?

- How might your congregation relate to a community partner or community initiative as part of the RElaunch strategy (i.e. local park revitalization, homeless population relief, elderly care, etc.)?

- Consider a week-long RElaunch with multiple touch points or a multi-weekend celebration building up to a big RElaunch.

- What is the intentional system to be used in any community activity to collect names? Is a team ready to respond and build relationships with the people whose names are collected? What is the multi-step process for follow-up, RElationship building, and opportunities for engagement?

- What is the communication strategy to let the neighborhood know the details about the RElaunch and invite them to be a part of it? How might the neighborhood be a part of the planning and preparing? Consider combinations of methods such as direct mail, door hangers, flyers, social media, boosted social media posts, website, local radio, local television, personal invitation, etc. Who is responsible for implementing the communication strategy? What is the timeline?

- How will the new relationships with the neighborhood play into the launch planning and implementation?

- What are the criteria or benchmarks that must be met in order to RElaunch (the non-negotiables? Consider such things as congregational REadiness to implement the RElaunch strategies, comprehensive dive into the RE Playbook with all REshapes complete, staff and/or ministry team leaders identified, equipped, in place and REady to implement the RElaunch plan.

- REsources (people, energy, commitment, dollars, equipment, etc.) in place to accommodate those ready to engage and take their first or next faithful steps (new small groups, new support groups, new affinity groups, new ministries, new serving opportunities, etc.)

- Asset alignment completed for RElaunch.

- Based on what you have learned and discovered in your work thus far in the REcalibrate, RElate, and REcommit portions of your RE Playbook, what style of worship would your targeted demographic in your mission field relate to most?

- Will you continue your online worship experience? Why or why not?

- Will you offer more than one worship experience? What brings you to this conclusion?

- What type of shifts need to be made in any existing worship experiences or ministries to better align with the strategic ministry plan for RElaunch?

- What type of extravagant hospitality would your targeted demographic most appreciate? Do you have a dedicated Hospitality Team trained and ready to serve?

- Are any REquired buildings and/ or grounds work completed?

- How are you preparing those who are already gathered for any changes they may experience from the way things used to be to the ways things are now in the life of their church?

- Are we confident that we are ready to offer our best and glorify God through our RElaunch?

RElaunch Playbook: RElaunch is not just about RE-opening the building for the same ol' worship service with those already gathered. RElaunch is full of potential if we invest wisely and strategically with time, commitment, resources, energy, and a heart for our neighbors.

RElaunch is a REintroduction of the faith community to the neighborhood. RElaunch is far beyond getting those already gathered back into the building to worship together. It is a part of the RElaunch, but it is not *the* RElaunch. If we think of the RElaunch as only "getting back to the way things should be," we will have completely missed the point, the opportunity, and a fleeting moment that will likely never come again in our lifetime. Too often we RElaunch prematurely without a RElaunch strategy or plan. It is better to postpone a RElaunch and do it well then to rush a RElaunch and do it poorly due to internal pressure from the already gathered.

This is your faith community's once-in-a-lifetime chance to REfresh, REnew, REvive, REform, REdesign, REclaim, REconnect, REshape, REfocus, REvision, and ultimately REjoice in how God can use us in new ways in this new day to reach new people!

RE Team REsponds

REflect

1. REflect on the checklist of considerations above for your RElaunch. Which of these of considerations were not on your radar, but should now be on your radar?

2. If you were to share with an already gathered congregant about why a RElaunch is important, how would you describe it?

3. How might the RElaunch plan be sabotaged? How will leaders prevent this from happening?

REveal

1. What key elements from the RElaunch consideration list must be a part of the RElaunch plan? Why?

2. What is the best timing for a RElaunch? What brings you to this conclusion?

3. Describe what God has REvealed to you as you have worked through the RE Playbook for RElaunch?

REshape to RElaunch

1. Name the RElaunch Team that needs to be gathered. What needs to be shared from the Playbook with this team?

2. How would you describe the non-negotiable priorities for the RElaunch?

3. What would be the markers for an effective and fruitful RElaunch?

A FINAL WORD

The RE Playbook has been created to help you REthink what it means to be the local church and how to show up differently in the community as both a faith community and as a disciple. It was meant to help you RE-prioritize the not yet gathered. The RE Playbook was intended to help you take the best advantage of the opportunity this horrible pandemic has provided. My prayer is that the RE Playbook will be used by the local church and through the guidance of the Holy Spirit, your church will RElaunch with a REnewed spirit, REinvigorated energy, and a REcommitment to being the church God is calling you to be, become, and do.

The RE Playbook is offered as a "bonus" to Being the Church in the Post Pandemic World. Once you have worked through the RE Playbook and successfully RElaunched your church into the community, the work is not over. Indeed, the work has only begun. Now is the time to dive deep into the book to further REdesign and REthink how to be the church in this post-pandemic world. I wish you well on your continued journey of faithful next steps in being the church for this new day!

Kay

Now is the time for your church to join us on...

Books
from Market Square
marketsquarebooks.com

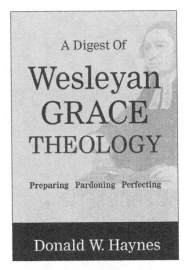

Wesleyan Grace Theology
Dr. Donald Haynes

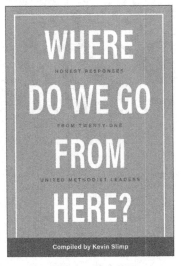

Where Do We Go From Here?
24 United Methodist Writers

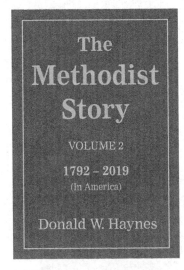

The Methodist Story Volume 2 ▪ 1792-2019
Dr. Donald W. Haynes

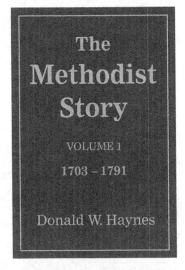

The Methodist Story Volume I ▪ 1703-1791
Dr. Donald Haynes

Grow Your Faith

with these books from Market Square

marketsquarebooks.com

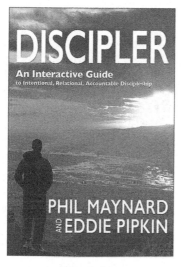

Discipler

Phil Maynard & Eddie Pipkin

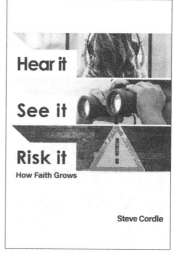

Hear It, See It, Risk It

Steve Cordle

A Christian Teenager's
Guide to Surviving High School

Ashley Conner

HOPE
An Advent Journey

Olu Brown

Be The Church

with these books from Market Square

marketsquarebooks.com

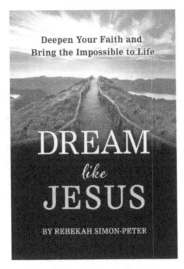

Dream Like Jesus
Bring the Impossible to Life
Rebekah Simon-Peter

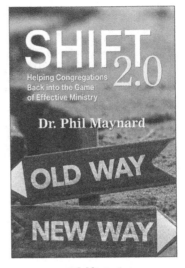

Shift 2.0
Phil Maynard

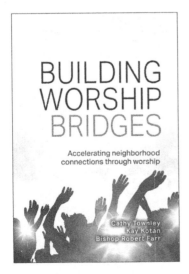

Building Worship
Bridges
Cathy Townley

Get Out of
That Box!
Anne Bosarge

Latest Titles
from Market Square Books
marketsquarebooks.com

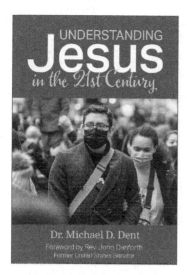

Understanding Jesus
in the 21st Century
Kay Kotan

**From Franchise
To Local Dive**
Jason Moore and Roz Picardo

Cultural Competency
Getting back into the venture with your neighbors
Paul Nixon

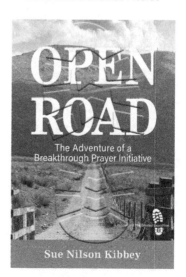

OPEN ROAD
Breakthrough Prayer Initiative
Sue Nilson Kibbey

More Books
from Market Square Books
marketsquarebooks.com

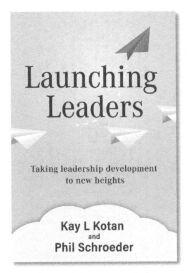

Launching Leaders
Leadership Development

Kay Kotan and Phil Schroeder

Tidings of Comfort and Joy

Charles W. Maynard

Mission Possible
Simple Structure for
Missional Effectiveness

Kay Kotan & Blake Bradford

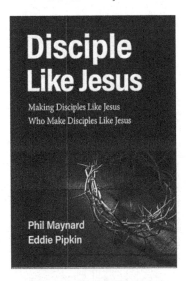

Disciple Like Jesus
Making Disciples Like Jesus
Who Make Disciples Like jesus

Phil Maynard & Eddie Pipkin

Made in the USA
Las Vegas, NV
08 May 2021